THE BEST GIFT

Sermons for the Advent, Christmas and Epiphany Seasons
Series A

John Thomas Randolph

0221/0-89536-617-7   PRINTED IN U.S.A.

*The book is dedicated to
David James
and
Harry Evans,
my brothers in the flesh,
my brothers in the ministry;
and
to
Joy Mae,
my sister,
whose life is a better sermon
than any I ever preached.*

TABLE OF CONTENTS

AN INVITATION

You are invited to "listen in" on the following sermons as they are being preached, primarily to my own congregation at the Mt. Olivet United Methodist Church in Seaford, Delaware.

It is difficult for me — in fact, nearly impossible — to write a book of sermons for an imaginary congregation of readers. But I enjoy writing sermons for the people I know and love in my own congregation. Therefore, these sermons were written and spoken with them in my mind. My guess is that you are not so different from my own people, so I am pleased to invite you to listen in on the sermons, in the hope that what was aimed at someone else will also be meaningful to you. So welcome, and come on in; the usher will show you to a seat!

Please do not be discouraged by the length of the sermons as they appear in this book. They are longer than I would actually preach in the context of a Sunday morning worship service. I tend to talk slowly and to ad lib comments, as the Spirit leads, when I preach, and it would probably take me forty minutes to preach some of the sermons in this book. The length of the printed sermons was determined by the publisher's request, but your reading speed should compensate for my speaking speed — and I promise not to ad lib while you are reading!

I hope my fairly frequent use of the personal pronoun does not make you uncomfortable. I am not an egotist, but I am sharing with you out of my own experience and to avoid the use of the personal pronoun would be both clumsy and misleading. The Christian sermon is a form of personal witness; it is a person standing in front of a congregation and declaring unashamedly, "This is what I believe."

If you find the sermons meaningful, then you will share my gratitude for Mrs. Joyce Stockslager, who typed the sermons for publication. Joyce's quiet competence has made my invitation to you possible.

I have asked the ushers to reserve one pew for some very special friends whose loving support has been a vehicle of God's grace and who have kept me going through some very difficult moments.

So come on in! The worship service has already begun, but you are just in time for the sermon.

John Thomas Randolph
Epiphany, 1983

Living Defensively

FIRST SUNDAY IN ADVENT
Matthew 24:37-44

I am tempted to begin this sermon by wishing you "A Happy New Year." This is the first Sunday in Advent, and Advent is the first season of the church year. In terms of the secular calendar, the first Sunday in Advent is not unlike the first day of January.

The theme of Advent is "Christ is coming!" The spirit of Advent is one of anticipation and preparation. Actually, Advent affirms the coming of Jesus Christ in three different but related tenses:

1. There is the past tense which refers to the actual historical birth of Jesus of Nazareth in the city of Bethlehem nearly two thousand years ago. Theologically, we refer to this event as the Incarnation.

2. There is the present tense in which the spirit of Christ enters into our own experience and comes alive there.

3. There is the future tense which is often referred to as the Parousia or "The Second Coming." That is, Christians believe that Jesus Christ is going to come back to earth at some unexpected time in the future.

I mention all this in order to put today's sermon in its proper perspective, for this particular sermon is going to be looking at the Parousia or the Second Coming of Christ.

As you may know, the State Police have a slogan which warns us to "Drive Defensively." It is based on the understanding that automobiles are dangerous weapons. We never know when another driver is going to lose control of his car or himself and swerve in front of us, creating a hazardous situation.

We may be riding along on a perfectly beautiful day, without a care in the world, when all of a sudden, another car may shoot out of a side road or cut across the median strip on the highway and crash right into us. It could happen so unexpectedly that we would never know what hit us. Therefore, our best protection against such a sudden and unexpected event is to "drive defensively." We actually drive as though we knew another car was going to pull out in front of us. Thus we are prepared to defend ourselves by responding in an appropriate manner.

All of this is relevant to today's Scripture lesson because Matthew 24:37-44 tells us to prepare for the Lord's coming by

Living Defensively

We do not know the day or the hour when Jesus Christ is going to return to the earth. A lot of people are guessing. It is a fairly frequent occurrence nowadays to hear someone announce that he knows the time. Not long ago, the planets aligned themselves in an unusual formation, and many people thought that event would mark the return of Christ to earth.

But all of the guessing is futile. In fact, Dr. William Barclay said it is nothing less than blasphemy. "Of that day and hour no one knows, not even the angels of heaven, nor the Son, but the Father only," writes Matthew. All we really know is that the coming of Christ is going to be as sudden and unexpected as an automobile shooting out in front of us from a side road. We had better be prepared by living defensively, for the situation will be potentially hazardous. For the Lord's coming will be accompanied by a time of judgment.

Those who have driven their lives well and have stayed on the main highway of God's will will be rewarded for their faithfulness. But those who have taken too many detours down the little sideroads of self-interest will be headed for a disappointing crash.

On the day when the Lord returns to earth in power and victory, "two men will be in the field and one will be taken and one will be left. Two women will be grinding at the mill and one will be taken and one will be left." That is the judgment, according to Matthew.

One day we will be going about our daily routine, and all of a sudden Jesus Christ will be standing right there beside us. I don't know what form he will take, but there will be no mistaking his presence. Somehow, we will know it is he, and though he may not speak a word to us, we will be judged.

Isn't that really the way judgment works? Fireworks aren't necessary. Planets do not have to line up in a particular order.

Suddenly greatness stands in our presence, and our own shortcomings become embarrassingly clear.

Christ-like love confronts us, and what we tried to pass off as love runs and hides its face.

Genuine holiness steps onto the scene and our sinfulness hightails it for cover.

A real craftsman drops into our workshop unexpectedly, and our piddling little efforts suddenly make us want to cry.

Just the presence of Christ — yea, even his loving presence — is just about all the judgment we can stand.

Several years ago, Dr. Charles L. Allen mailed out thousands of small billfold size pictures of Christ. He received hundreds of letters from the satisfied recipients. One man wrote that he had lost his billfold with a large amount of money in it. A few days later he received it in the mail with a note from the finder which said, "When I first found this, I fully intended to keep the money. But when I looked at that picture of Christ, I had to send it back."

This is the judgment. Even the *picture* of Christ does something to us.

The One who is coming will stand in our presence, and all of us, and our work and our play and our relationships will be called into account. We don't know exactly when that will happen so we are wise if we live defensively.

Matthew 24:37-44 continues to be helpful at this point because it suggests that

The Best Defense Is a Good Offense

Now this is the language of the athletic field. While I have never been a great athlete, I have been interested in sports long enough to know that this is true: The best defense *is* a good offense.

The best way for the Baltimore Orioles to defend themselves against the hitting prowess of the Chicago White Sox is for the Orioles to make a lot of runs first. The best way for the Dallas Cowboys to defend themselves against the scoring power of the Pittsburgh Steelers is for the Cowboys to score a lot of touchdowns first. The best way to avoid being hit by another driver is to drive your own car carefully and responsibly.

The practical bottom line is that we must live all of life as a continuous preparation for the Lord's coming. That is what you call "running a good offense." If you are successful at it, it will defend you from a lot of tragedy and heartache when the time of judgment comes.

Noah defended himself and his family by running a good offense. He prepared his boat when the weather was calm and the sun was shining, and, therefore, he was ready when the flood came.

Too often we wait until the crisis comes before we

even begin to prepare, and by that time it may be too late. You may remember that old song about the fellow who had a hole in his roof, but he never got around to repairing it. Why? Because when it was raining, he couldn't repair it. When the sun was shining, he saw no need to repair it.

Obviously, the time to prepare for a crisis is now, when things seem to be running along relatively smoothly. The time to prepare for Christ's coming is right now.

This is one of the main values of Advent: It focuses our attention on the need to prepare.

The householder must assume that his house will be broken into every night or else he will procrastinate in taking the necessary security precautions. Indeed, from a practical point of view, we know that even taking precautions will not completely save us from burglary. I am reminded of the man in Massachusetts who bought a watchdog to protect his valuable paintings. But in the morning, his paintings were gone and the watchdog was sound asleep on the kitchen floor! As a general rule, however, it does help us to take precautions against the unexpected appearance of thieves.

You see, there is an urgency to our preparation for the coming of Christ. We cannot afford to hesitate. This is illustrated by a fable about three apprentice devils who were talking to Satan, the chief of devils, about their plans to destroy humankind.

The first apprentice suggested that they destroy man by telling him there is no God. Satan rejected that suggestion because he realized that most people knew there was a God and would not be convinced otherwise.

The second apprentice suggested that they destroy man by telling him there is no hell. Satan also rejected this suggestion because he knew that too many people could not be convinced that there was no hell.

Finally, the third apprentice said, "Let us destroy

man by telling him there is no hurry!" Satan loved that suggestion because he knew that people would believe there was no hurry and they would be destroyed by the thousands.

Perhaps the most dangerous of all delusions is that there is plenty of time to prepare for the Lord's coming.

We must prepare now. We must get our lives into order now. We must reaffirm our Christian commitment now. These are things that cannot be put off because no person can be completely certain that there will even be a tomorrow for him or her.

I don't mean to be gloomy, but there is a realistic urgency about our preparation for the coming of Christ.

When we come right down to it, the best offense, the best preparation, is to live every day *as though* it were our last.

John Wesley, the founder of The Methodist Church, gave us a good example of this kind of living. A woman had asked Wesley, "Supposing that you knew you were to die at 12 o'clock tomorrow night. How would you spend the intervening time?"

Wesley replied: "How Madam? Why just as I intend to spend it now. I should preach this evening at Gloucester and again at five tomorrow morning; after that I should ride to Tewkesbury, preach in the afternoon and meet the society in the evening; I should then repair to friend Martin's house, who expects to entertain me, converse and pray with the family as usual; retire at 10 o'clock, commend myself to my heavenly Father; lie down to rest and wake up in glory."

You can't go wrong with an approach like that! That is what you call running a great offense. That is waiting for the Lord's coming, in the most positive and constructive manner possible. That is waiting for the Lord's return, yet doing it in a way that is watchful and alert and ever open to new opportunities to serve him.

Let us seek to live this way as we use the Advent

season as a time to prepare for the coming of Jesus Christ into the world and into our own lives.

Just one final note: As you get into your car and leave the church building today, remember to "Drive Defensively!"

Someone Is Shouting

SECOND SUNDAY IN ADVENT
Matthew 3:1-12

Traditionally, Advent has been thought of as a rather solemn period of preparation for the coming of Christ. It is the time when we get ready for the deepest meaning of Christmas. We ask ourselves significant questions. Who is the One whose birthday we will celebrate? What is his relationship to us and to our world? Will the spirit of one who was born nearly two thousand years ago on the first Christmas be reborn within us this Christmas? How can we help the rebirth of the Christ spirit to happen?

These are serious questions, the kinds of questions we need to take with us into a quiet place for prayerful consideration. That is why Advent has been thought of as a time for solemn and sober reflection.

But today, this quiet solemnity is broken. The silence is pierced by a shout!

There is a new preacher in town, and his name is John the Baptizer. Matthew says that he came in fulfillment of Isaiah's prophecy that "Someone is shouting in the desert, 'Prepare a road for the Lord.' " Before John has opened his mouth more than three or four times, it is clear that he is a member of the "old school" of shouting evangelists who were known largely because of their volume. No doubt about it. John was a shouter. The question is: Why did John shout?

John Shouted in Order to Be Heard

There is so much noise in the world today. There are so many voices competing for our attention. If you want to be heard, you almost have to shout.

I have read that during a typical lunch hour at the University of California at Berkeley, spokesmen for a dozen different causes can be found on the plaza, trying to outshout one another. One day a lone figure sat down defiantly in the middle of the crowd and held up a sign which said, "SILENT PROTEST." Someone tapped him on the shoulder and asked, "What are you protesting?" The defiant figure held up another sign which said simply, "NOISE."

That experience reminds me of the Salvation Army lassie who was informed by a policeman that a local ordinance would prevent her from ringing her bells to invite contributions. But such a crude law could not stop such an inventive woman. The next day she did a brisker business than ever as she waved one sign and then another in the air. The signs said "ding" and "dong."

There is so much noise in the world, especially in these days that lead up to Christmas — music blaring out of every store; impatient customers raising their voices to get the attention of overworked store clerks; the sound of horns and traffic jams. If you really want to be heard in the midst of all this noise, you are probably going to have to shout.

I am not trying to say that John the Baptizer had to contend with all the noise that characterizes our preparation for Christmas in the 1980's. But noise is nothing new. There has always been noise when the spokesmen for diverse causes were competing for the attention of an audience. At least this is why I believe that one of the reasons John shouted was simply to be heard.

Of course, there is an added reason to shout if you are

an eccentric as John was! Someone wearing clothes made of camel's hair and leather girdle around his waist is not exactly the kind of fellow who is going to be invited to give an interview on the "Today" program. "That's Incredible" — maybe. But not "Today." Governors and Presidents are not going to seek him out in order to learn his point of view. In fact, the Secret Service Agents would probably haul him in for questioning!

People like John have to shout and then just hope that someone hears them.

John Also Shouted Because He Was Angry

At least, he strikes me as being angry. A person does not usually go around calling respectable citizens "a brood of vipers" or "snakes" unless he is angry. A person does not usually liken other people to trees that ought to be cut down unless he is at least halfway mad.

Just the other day, I took my typewriter into a local repair shop to have the electric carriage return fixed. When I went to pick it up, I found that the shop had assumed the prerogative of rebuilding the whole machine, or so it seemed to me at the time. The bill was $72.75. On top of that revolting development, the shop would not permit me to charge the repair job to the church and take the typewriter home with me. I was told that I had to pay in cash. I didn't have it. The church treasurer was out of town. My wife was thirty miles away with our checkbook.

Well, friends, I'll tell you I was angry, and I shouted. I don't think it did much good, but I shouted. I tried to restrain myself in public places, but when I got out into the open, I shouted.

John shouted when he got angry, too. Only he had a more legitimate cause for his anger. Basically, he was angry at sin!

He fearlessly denounced it whenever and wherever he

found it. He wasn't any respecter of rank or status. John got angry at Herod the King when he married an unlawful wife. John got angry at the leading churchmen of his day when they sank into ritualistic formalism. He even got angry at ordinary people who were living lives that were unaware of God. John denounced sin and evil in the state, in the church, in the crowd, and wherever else he found it. "Sin is sin," he shouted. "Turn away from it!"

It is interesting to note the contrast between the approach of John and the approach of Jesus. Jesus, too, called people away from their sin, but he did it quietly and lovingly. To be sure, Jesus could get angry, but anger for him was the exception and not the rule. For John, anger appeared to be the rule.

In any case, I believe that is one of the reasons John shouted. He shouted because he was angry.

Finally, John Shouted to Accentuate His Message

When your message is not popular, people do not flock to hear it. In fact, they run in the opposite direction! If you want your message to be heard, then you have to shout it. It is like using a highpowered drill to penetrate an object of heavy resistance.

John's message of repentance was not popular. "Repent!" he said. "Turn away from your sins," he shouted. He had to shout it loud enough to be heard by people who were running away from him.

I used to live near Dover, Delaware, and had to go to that lovely city on many occasions. I will never forget a man who dressed in old raggedy clothes and used to walk up and down Loockerman Street and through the parking lot of the shopping mall, shouting out one word over and over again. "Repent!" he would shout. Then, going on a few more steps, he would shout it out again: "Repent!" It was almost as though John the Baptizer had come to life in our own time. To all appearances, no one paid much attention to this fellow either.

Now the problem with repentance, as I understand it, is that no one knows or cares very much what it means.

For example, in John Steinbeck's story of *The Wayward Bus,* a dilapidated old bus takes a cross-country shortcut on its journey from Rebel Corners to Los Angeles and gets stuck in the mud. While the driver goes for assistance, the passengers take refuge in a cave.

They form a curious company. There is a girl who danced at stag parties, a traveling salesman out for laughs, a boy named Pimple who is girl crazy, and a shallow-principled businessman with his repressed wife and free-thinking daughter. It appears clear that Steinbeck intended these characters to represent a lot of people in our society who are "lost" spiritually as well as physically.

The cave in which they take refuge has one word written over it in black paint: "REPENT!" A wandering preacher had gone to a lot of trouble to paint the word there as his way of "spreading God's word in a sinful world." And here is the thing I want you to notice: The only one to even notice the word is the businessman, and the only reason he noticed it is because he wondered who had financed such a venture.

Does anyone besides the theologians know what it means to repent? Does anyone care?

For the purpose of this sermon, I have to assume that you, at least, are interested in what repentance means. As I understand it, repentance means that a person undergoes a complete interior change of heart, a total renewal of spirit, and the adoption of a whole new outlook and attitude.

Repentance is more than the desire, even the sincere desire, to "change our ways." I am thinking now of a young woman who stopped to use the church telephone one day. I had assisted her on two or three previous occasions. She used the telephone to call the state prison to make arrangements to visit her husband who was an inmate there. As she waited to be connected with the visiting room at the prison, she brought me up to date on what had been happening to her: "I've really learned my lesson, Reverend. Being in prison for six months — I just got out last week — has changed me. I don't know why I always get into such messes, but it just seems to happen. But I'm cured now, Reverend, I've changed my ways!"

How wonderful, I thought, the dear girl has really repented.

But just the other day, I read that she was arrested for cutting a hole in the prison fence and trying to help her husband escape. She vowed and declared to the authorities that she was not trying to get her husband *out.* She was only trying to get herself *in* so she could visit him. I don't know why the police insist on being so skeptical and simply refuse to believe her story!

Repentance, you see, is more than *saying* that we have learned our lesson and changed our ways. Repentance is being so sorry about something that we actually quit it! Repentance is doing an "about face" away from everything that separates us from God and, in the process, turning toward him.

It is, as we said earlier, undergoing a complete interior change of heart, a total renewal of spirit, and adopting a whole new outlook and attitude.

Experiencing such repentance may be the best way for us to prepare for Christmas.

If we listen carefully, we will hear it even above the other holiday noises. Someone is shouting: Turn away from your sins and turn toward the God who is coming to meet us in Jesus Christ, our Lord.

Is Christ the One?

THIRD SUNDAY IN ADVENT
Matthew 11:2-11

Bishop Herbert Welch was one of the most remarkable persons in the history of the United Methodist Church. He lived to be one-hundred-and-six years old and maintained an active schedule into his one hundred-and-third year. On one occasion, late in his life, he was to speak to a church congregation that had never met him. An officer of the church was sent to the airport to greet the visiting bishop.

Aware of Welch's age, the officer kept looking for an old man to step down from the plane. Welch was such an athletic and youthful-looking person, however, that he passed by the church officer who never even noticed him. It must have been an embarrassing experience for the officer. In my mind's eye, which is colored by today's Scripture lesson, I can see him standing there by the airplane, and every time an elderly gentleman left the plane, he asked himself: "Is he the one who is to come, or shall I look for another?"

That was basically the same question that John the Baptizer asked of Jesus. It was a different situation, of course, but the same question. People had been looking forward to the coming of the Messiah for years. Then John appeared and told the people to get ready for the Lord's coming. There is no doubt in my mind that John was convinced that Jesus was the long-expected Messiah. But time passed and some things happened and some things didn't happen, and now John was in prison. We will never know exactly what was going on in his mind, but he sent some of his disciples to Jesus with this question: "Are you he who is to come, or shall we look for another?"

It is a good question. It is a good question for us during this Advent season. Some of us have been looking for years for someone who would give meaning and purpose to life. We have been looking for someone who would heal our brokenness, as individuals and as nations. We have been looking for someone who would bring the dead back to life again — both the "living dead" and the literally dead. We have been looking for someone who would introduce some good news into a world that is filled with so much bad news.

Now Advent tells us that Christ is coming, and John the Baptizer's question becomes our own: "Is Jesus the one we have been looking for, or shall we look for another?" You will not be surprised, will you, that this sermon will answer the question affirmatively. Yes, my friends, Christ is the one we have been looking for. The "evidence" for our positive answer is based upon today's Scripture lesson. So, to begin,

The Witness of John Himself says "Yes"

The overwhelming weight of John's witness affirms that Jesus is the one we have been looking for. True, it was John who raised the question in the first place, but it was raised only after John had invested a great deal of his life in giving a positive answer to the question.

Indeed, our major tip-off that Jesus was the Messiah was John's preparation for his coming. "Prepare the way of the Lord, make his paths straight," shouted John (Mark 1:3). Then, John nearly refused to baptize Jesus, saying that it was Jesus who should be baptizing him (Matthew 3:14). It certainly seems clear that John was personally convinced that Jesus was the Messiah, the Christ, the "Coming One."

So, someone asks, if John was so sure that Jesus was the one that people had been looking for, why did he raise the question? I must answer, I am not sure. The question may have been prompted by the crisis he was in. You will remember that John was in prison when he asked the question. His death was not far away. It may be that in those final difficult and dark days in a dungeon, John simply wanted one last, direct confirmation of the faith for which he was dying.

That would be understandable. I really do believe in life after death, but if I raise a question about it as I lay dying, do not be critical of me for having "doubts." Instead, please humor me and do me the honor of confirming my faith! I think I can understand John's question and his reason for asking it. Can't you?

In any case, I do know this: Those who raise the hardest questions about a cause are often the staunchest advocates of that cause. For example, I have just been reading John Holt's book, *Escape From Childhood.* Some of the most difficult and challenging questions that I have ever heard about childhood are raised by Holt. But, at the same time, it is quite clear that children have few advocates who are more dedicated or intelligent than John Holt.

John the Baptizer raised the question that is the basis of this sermon, but his own life and witness are a very positive answer to that question. Yes — Jesus Christ is the one we have been looking for.

The Works of Jesus Also Say "Yes"

It is significant that Jesus did not give a direct answer to John's question, "Are you the one?" Rather, he said, "Go and tell John what you hear and see: the blind receive their sight and the lame walk, lepers are cleansed and the deaf hear, and the dead are raised up, and the poor have good news preached to them." (Matthew 11:4) In other words, Jesus was saying, "Go back to John, but do not tell him what I am saying; tell him what I am doing. Do not tell John what I am claiming, but tell him what is happening."

For Jesus, the acid test was always the test of action. He never was very impressed with what we say. He always was more impressed by what we do. Christians are known by their fruits, he said (John 15:1-11). True prophets can be distinguished from false prophets because what true prophets say actually happens, he said. And Jesus said, "Not every one who says to me 'Lord, Lord,' shall enter the kingdom of heaven, but he who does the will of my Father who is in heaven." (Matthew 7:21)

So when Simon Peter professed that he loved Jesus, Jesus told him, "Feed my sheep." (John 21:15-23) In fact, Jesus told him basically the same thing three times! The point is that Jesus was always interested in what others were actually *doing,* in what was *happening* in their lives. For him, that was the acid test.

It is to the credit of Jesus, therefore, that he applied the same test to himself. "Go and tell John what is happening as a result of my ministry. Don't tell him what I am saying. Tell him what I am doing — tell him what God is doing for others through me, and what is being done for others can also be done for you."

One of my favorite songs, back in the 1950's, was "It Is No Secret What God Can Do." It was written and sung by Stuart Hamblen. There is an interesting story behind that song.

Hamblen was a disc-jockey in Los Angles in 1949, at the time of the first big Billy Graham Crusade. He had developed a serious drinking problem that was destroying his life, but after several visits to the Crusade meetings, his life was radically changed. We would say that he was converted. Damaging, old temptations left him, and new, creative affections took charge of his life. A friend who heard that Stuart had not touched a drop of alcohol for thirty days said to him, "Tell me truthfully, Stuart, have you wanted one drink?" The answer was as direct as the question: "No, John. It is no secret what God can do." "You ought to write a song about what God can do," said John. Stuart wrote the song, and that is how many of us have come to sing, "It is no secret what God can do. What He's done for others, He'll do for you."

You see, God through Jesus Christ is still bringing good news to the poor. He is still bringing those who were dead back to life again! He is still healing those who were broken!

In the May, 1982, issue of *Guideposts* magazine, Norman Vincent Peale tells of a woman who came to him for help. Her husband had been killed in a tragic car crash, and as a result, she felt numb, hopeless, and broken.

Peale was able to help her by telling her a true story about a distinguished British violinist named Peter Cropper. Cropper's work was so outstanding that the Royal Academy of Music in London had honored him by lending him a priceless 258-year old Stradivarius. It is the dream of every violinist to be able to play such an instrument! But a terrible thing happened while Cropper was performing in Finland. He tripped and fell on top of the Stradivarius and broke it. Cropper's pleasant dream was turned into a horrible nightmare. He was inconsolable.

Then a London violin dealer told him of a master craftsman who could repair the Stradivarius. To make a long story short, the repairs were so perfect they could not even be seen, and the soaring notes of the instrument were more beautiful than they had ever been before — all because the broken parts were placed in the hands of a master craftsman who then applied his healing touch.

Yes, Jesus Christ is the one we have been looking for. Something terrible happens and our lives are broken. Then we turn them over to Jesus Christ who is the Master Craftsman of all time. He takes the broken pieces and puts them back together again, and we are better than new!

So go tell John and anyone else who will listen: The works of Jesus, what he is actually doing for us and others, affirm that he is the one we are looking for. There is no need to look "for another."

And, finally,

The Words of Jesus Say "Yes" — He Is the One

I must explain what I mean here or you may think that I am contradicting what has already been said. I have already said that Jesus did not use words, directly, to affirm that he was the Messiah. He let his works or actions serve as his main vehicle of communication. But *indirectly*, his words clearly indicated that he did see himself as the Messiah, the Christ, the one the people had been looking for.

For example, when Jesus told John's disciples to go back and to tell John that "the poor were having good news preached to them," he was affirming indirectly that he was the Messiah. For Jesus was describing that particular activity in the language of Isaiah 61:1 which was considered messianic in nature. Preaching to the poor was an accepted sign of the messianic age. John the Baptizer would have known that, and Jesus knew that John would know that!

What we are saying, most simply, is this: Jesus did use his words to communicate, *indirectly*, that he was the one whom we have been looking for!

Let us conclude this sermon with an incident in *Alice in Wonderland.* One of the characters in that marvelous story is a lock. The lock is very restless and can not be still for a single moment. It is obviously hunting for something as it looks behind every rock and tree. As Alice watches the lock, her curiosity is aroused and she asks, "What is the matter?" The lock replies, "I am looking for something to unlock me."

To me, that incident represents the bottom line to this sermon. Along with John and millions of others, we have been looking for someone to bring us good news and to heal our brokenness and to give us new life. Well, there is no need to go on searching "for another." Christ is the one we were looking for. It is he who unlocks the meaning and purpose of life!

That's Incredible!

FOURTH SUNDAY IN ADVENT
Matthew 1:18-25

SPECIAL ANNOUNCEMENT

TO: The Whole World

FROM: Mary and Joseph

Mary is going to have a baby. We invite you to join us next Sunday in celebrating this happy event.

Joseph learned of the birth from an angel of the Lord in a dream.

The angel told Joseph not be afraid, that the baby would be conceived by the Holy Spirit, that his name would be called Jesus, and that he would also be known as Emmanuel.

Please join us in our Christmas celebration!

Regrets only.

Now, that is incredible!

I believe that this "special announcement" is an accurate summary of today's Scripture lesson, and it is absolutely incredible.

I am aware that there is a television program called "That's Incredible," but it reports events that are relatively tame by comparison. The television program may tell us about a motorcyclist who can jump his motorcycle over twenty-five busses, or a man who can extinguish a forest fire with his bare hands, or a woman who has fingernails that are thirty feet long. But these events are rather ordinary when compared with the special announcement that is reported in today's Scripture lesson. The announcement is incredible for several reasons.

To begin, it is

Incredible in Its Origin

The original announcement that Mary was going to have a baby was made by an angel of the Lord.

I have heard many announcements that babies were going to be born, but they were usually made by expectant mothers or proud fathers-to-be or grandparents or doctors. I have never heard, or heard of, an angel announcing that a baby was going to be born. Of course, what Matthew is saying is that it was God himself who made it known to Joseph that Mary was going to have a baby.

God made this information known to Joseph in a dream.

If I remember correctly, the psychologist Sigmund Freud referred to dreams as "the royal road to the unconscious." He believed that the memory of unpleasant experiences was repressed or pushed down beneath the level of conscious awareness. When we sleep, however, we "let our guard down" so to speak, and these unpleasant memories rise to the level of our awareness. Thus, according to Freud, you can tell a lot about a person by interpreting his dreams.

I can understand that. It sounds like a perfectly

logical and rational analysis. There is nothing incredible about it.

But for Joseph to get — through a dream — his first knowledge that his own "wife" was pregnant — well, that is incredible!

I have heard of people who claimed to be able to predict the future through dreams. I have known people who said that they received great insights through dreams. I have even had a few interesting dreams myself. But I have never heard of anyone, until Joseph, who learned through a dream that his wife was going to have a baby.

So, the announcement to Joseph was incredible in its origin: It came from God in a dream.

From now on, perhaps we should pay more attention to our dreams. But more important, we have gained an insight into the fact that all great announcements have, or should have, their origins in God. If a man and woman are going to announce their marriage, they had better be sure that that event had its origin in their relationship with God. If a person is about to announce his decision to enter a particular vocation, he had better double check to see that his decision originated in his relationship with God. If a country is considering an increase in its military budget while at the same time it is cutting back on its budget for human services, it had better ask itself if its decision is rooted in an understanding of what is God's will for that country.

We do not always learn of great events through dreams, but all truly great events do have their origins in God and our relationship with him.

Second, the announcement to Joseph was

Incredible in Its Contents

1. Can you imagine that after the angel told Joseph that Mary was going to have a baby, the angel actually

told Joseph "not to be afraid!" That is incredible when you stop to consider the circumstances, because according to the customs of that place and time, Joseph had very good reason to be afraid.

According to the normal Jewish procedure of that day, the marriage relationship involved three stages. There was an engagement period, a betrothal, and the marriage proper.

The engagement was arranged for the couple to be married by the parents or a matchmaker and lasted for a year. At the end of a year, the girl could choose not to continue any further in the relationship. However, if she chose to continue the relationship, the couple became betrothed. They were looked upon at this point as husband and wife and their relationship could only be terminated by a divorce. But there was this important difference — they were not permitted to have any intimate relations that could lead to the birth of a child. If the woman became pregnant during the year of betrothal, before the marriage proper took place, it was bad news for the man. For he was subject to very severe penalties.

That is precisely the predicament that Joseph was in! Mary was going to have a baby during the year of betrothal, and Joseph had good reason to be afraid. Yet, the angel tells Joseph, "do not be afraid." Any sensible man would be frightened out of his skin, or so we might think.

2. Joseph is not supposed to be afraid because Mary is going to have her baby through the power of the Holy Spirit.

We call it the virgin birth, and it is one of the most incredible ideas that was ever introduced to the world. Many of us may accept the virgin birth of Jesus on the basis of biblical authority, but we do not understand it.

I have a beautiful little friend in the seventh grade whose name is Kristin. She is a very bright and sensitive girl, but she does not understand everything she hears in church. (I am sure that many of us can identify with that!) One day when Kristin was in the cafeteria at school, one of her curious friends asked her, "Are you a virgin?" Well, Kristin was really on the spot because she did not know what a virgin was. But she did some quick thinking that went like this: The only virgin she had heard of was Mary, and everyone knows that Mary had a baby. Therefore, a virgin must be a woman who has had a baby.

Thus armed with that conclusion, Kristin announced loudly to her friend in the cafeteria, "No! I am not a virgin!" As several people nearby registered their shock, one little boy leaned over and whispered in her ear: "Kristin, I don't think you know what you are talking about!"

Many of us, adults included, do not know what we are talking about when we are talking about the virgin birth, but as I understand it, the virgin birth *means* that Jesus came from God. He is God's Son. The emphasis is not primarily on Mary, but on the creative life-giving power of Almighty God. As Reginald H. Fuller, the theologian, expresses it, Jesus is not the product of human evolution, the highest achievement of the human race, but he is the product of the intervention of a transcendent God into human history.

Now — that is incredible!

I believe that the creative power of God is involved in every human birth, and the birth of every child is a miracle. The whole birth process is an absolutely incredible process, and this only makes me appreciate all the more the unique way in which Jesus is the Son of God.

The contents of the birth announcement were incredible in that they told Joseph not to be afraid when it appeared that he had good reason to be afraid and they told Joseph that the baby would be born to a virgin.

3. It was also incredible that the name of the baby was to be called Jesus, which means that he will save his people from their sins.

That is some claim to make for a baby! While I am tempted to run ahead in the story and to say a lot of theological things about how that baby grew up and gave himself in suffering love on behalf of sinful humankind, thus restoring us to fellowship with God, let me stay on the idea of the saving power of a baby.

Harry Emerson Fosdick told the story of General Pickett's baby. It was during the last slaughterous days of the Civil War when the Confederates locked horns with the Union soldiers outside of Richmond. It was the cruelest time of the whole war. Then one night the Confederate lines were lighted with bonfires, and the Union guards discovered that the Southern troops were celebrating General Pickett's newborn baby, word of whose arrival had just reached the army. General Grant was so moved by the event that he ordered the Union lines to help the Confederates celebrate the birth of Pickett's baby by lighting up the scene with additional bonfires.

The next day Grant's officers sent a graceful letter through the lines under a flag of truce, communicating to General Pickett the congratulations of his enemies!

Isn't that incredible?

For a moment, at least, the insanity and slaughter of war stopped, and good will and peace prevailed — and it was all because of a baby!

We cannot hear that story and not think of the baby who was born in Bethlehem. "His name will be called Jesus," announced the angel, "for he will save his people from their sins." We cannot draw closer to the Christ-child without also drawing closer to God, his Father, and as we draw closer to God, our sinfulness decreases and the spirit of peace and goodwill toward others and God increases.

It is incredible, but it is true.

4. Then the contents of the announcement tell us that Jesus will also be known as Emmanuel, which means God is with us.

God has come to be with us through Jesus, the one whose birthday we will celebrate at Christmas. God will be with us through our good times and our bad times, through our days of health and our days of illness, through our days of joy and our days of sorrow, through our days of winning and our days of losing. It is a most incredible promise, but one that millions of persons have found to be true.

Don Pooley is a professional golfer. He is not a superstar like Jack Nicklaus, and he has to struggle to qualify to play in the major tournaments. He has always thought that it was God's will for his life that he should be a golfer. He worked hard to use the skills and opportunities that God had given him. But he was having a difficult time, not even winning enough prize money to pay his bills.

He began to doubt that God wanted him to be a golfer, and began to consider some other options. But that made him even more frustrated and unhappy. Finally, he made a new commitment to the Lord and asked for his presence with him on the golf course. He began to play with a newfound sense of peace and patience and concentration and confidence. Then, in the B.C. Open Golf Tournament in 1980, he found himself in a tough situation where if he made a difficult putt, he would win his first major competition. Ordinarily, he would have panicked, but now, he stepped away from the ball and prayed silently: "Thank you, Lord, for always being here, even when I forget, and for providing me what I need right here." He made the putt and he won the tournament.

I am not trying to say that if you pray, then you are going to be a championship golfer. But what I want you to notice and believe is this: If we try to stay within the will of God for our lives, then God is always present with us no matter where we are — even on a golf course! And even when we forget!

It is really incredible.

The baby who was conceived by the Holy Spirit and born to Mary, the same baby who was called Jesus because he would save his people from their sins, is also to be known as Emmanuel, because through him and his spirit, the Almighty God of the universe is present with us in all times and in all places.

The angel's announcement that Mary would bear a son was incredible, both in its origin and in its contents.

And finally,

Joseph's Response to the Announcement Was Also Incredible

He complied with it. He obeyed God. "He did as the angel of the Lord commanded him; he took his wife, but knew her not until she had borne a son; and he called his name Jesus."

In light of the circumstances we have already mentioned, it really is incredible that Joseph obeyed the command of the Lord! He could have fled the country and no one would have blamed him! He not only obeyed, but he did it graciously. He treated Mary with sensitivity and compassion.

No announcement is complete until it has received a response. With Joseph's obedient response, the angel's announcement was complete. Almost.

Joseph made his response, but what about us? What is our personal response to the annoucement?

It would seem that our response should follow Joseph's example. That is, we should respond obediently to the will of God as we perceive his will — no matter how incredible his will appears to be, either in origin or content.

We should celebrate. We should celebrate the most incredible birth of the most incredible Person who ever lived. We should celebrate every day. But there will be special joy in the celebration just one week from today, on Christmas!

The Best Gift

CHRISTMAS
Luke 2:1-20

It's a wonderful thing when Christmas falls on Sunday as it does this year. It makes for a hectic schedule, but most of us would agree it is worth it. Only an hour or two ago, some of you were still unwrapping your presents.

I would like to ask you a question: What is the very best gift you received this year? Was it a special article of clothing? Was it a toy like a "choo-choo train that really goes"? Was it a car? Was it a diamond engagement ring? Was it simply the fact that a loved one got home for the holidays? Or was it something else? What is the best gift that you received for Christmas?

I have saved a newspaper clipping from 1977. It tells us that the best gift that Jack Millikan received for Christmas that year was the return of his dog, Jesse. Jack had an accident in June of that year, and Jesse, who was with him, was injured and ran away. Six months and six hundred-fifty miles later, Jesse made it back home. The headline of the newspaper account says, "Dog's Gift Is Herself." Jack Millikan's best gift that Christmas was Jesse's gift of herself.

I'd like to suggest that the best gift we have received this Christmas is God's gift of himself. "The word became flesh and dwelt among us," is the way John's Gospel expresses it (1:14). Luke expresses it this way: "And the angel said . . ., 'Behold, I bring you good news of a great joy which will come to all the people; for to you is born this day . . . a Savior, who is Christ the Lord.' " (2:10,11) This is what Christmas is all about: God gives himself to us in the form of his Son, Jesus Christ. God gives us many things, of course, but the best gift is the gift of himself.

To call something "the best gift" is to make quite a claim for it, and in order to deserve that title, a gift must meet at least three basic criteria: it must not wear out; we must be able to take it with us wherever we go, and we must be able to share it.

God's Gift of Himself Will Not Wear Out

It's the only gift I know of that doesn't rust, rot, or fade away. I dare say that some of the toys that the children received this morning are already broken. I think the best gift I ever received as a boy was a bicycle — a very special bicycle. A Western Flyer! Red and white! Colored streamers on the handle grips! But in time it wore out and ended up on the junk heap. All the material gifts we receive eventually endure the same fate.

In fact, some manufacturers actually plan for their products to wear out. We call it "planned obsolescence." Then the consumer is forced to buy a replacement. Material gifts, therefore, may bring us temporary pleasure, but they are not the best gifts because they do not last very long.

I was talking with a friend the other day who recently retired from the DuPont Company here in Seaford. You all know, of course, that Seaford, Delaware, is known as "The Nylon Capitol of the World." My friend was telling me that nylon is one of the most durable products that is made by man. It is possible to make a pair of nylon stockings which, for all practical purposes, would never wear out. However, that would require making the individual strands of the stocking so thick that most women would consider them unattractive. In other words, the vanity of the purchaser requires the manufacturer to make the nylon stockings so sheer that they will, in fact, wear out — sometimes very quickly. (Such is the price of vanity!)

While I was preparing this sermon, the newspapers announced that Sachel Paige had died. Leroy (Sachel) Paige was one of the most effective and colorful baseball pitchers who ever lived. You may remember him for his famous saying, "Don't look back, something may be gaining on you." Paige did not pitch in the major leagues until he was forty-two, but then he went on to pitch in the major leagues for several more years. The amazing thing is that Paige did not even begin to pitch in the major leagues until he was well past the age when most baseball players retire! In 1965, at the age of fifty-eight, he signed a contract to begin playing for the Kansas City Athletics. No one really knew how old Sachel Paige was when he died. I am sure that many baseball fans thought he would never die, but eventually, like all of us, he did "wear out."

God's Christmas gift of himself is the only thing that doesn't wear out. Jesus Christ is "the same yesterday, today, and tomorrow." He comes with a billion-year-plus warranty. He is guaranteed by God to last forever. He is one of the few gifts that will outlast us. For as Isaiah puts it: "The grass withers, the flower fades; but the word of God will stand forever." (40:8)

Henry Lyte expressed it poetically in his hymn which draws a contrast between a changing world and a changeless God:

Swift to its close ebbs out life's little day;
Earth's joys grow dim; its glories pass away;
Change and decay in all around I see;
O Thou who changest not, abide with me.

God's gift of himself, through Jesus Christ, is the best gift we have ever received because he can be experienced for a whole lifetime — and beyond.

We never tire of the Christmas story as it is recorded in the second chapter of the Gospel of Luke. It is so tremendous and durable because it tells us of a gift that will never wear out!

God's Gift of Himself Is Also the Best Gift Because He Can Be Taken With Us Wherever We Go

One of the problems with my bicycle was that it could not be put into the car and taken with us when we went to visit friends in another town. It was too clumsy and bulky. Sometimes a pocket knife or a doll makes a better gift than something that is much larger and more expensive, because we can take those things with us wherever we go.

In order for something to qualify as "the best gift," it has to be equally applicable and meaningful in all kinds of situations no matter where we are. In the final analysis, no material gift can meet this criterion, because as the old saying goes, "You can't take it with you when you go."

Jesus Christ is the best gift because he is always with us. In fact, one of the names given to Jesus was "Emmanuel," which means "God is with us." No matter where we are, God is present. No matter where we go, God goes with us.

When I was growing up in the church, we used to sing an old hymn by Lydia Baxter:

Take the name of Jesus with you,
child of sorrow and of woe;
It will joy and comfort give you;
take it, then, where'er you go.

> *Take the name of Jesus ever,*
> *as a shield from every snare;*
> *If temptations round you gather,*
> *breathe that holy name in prayer.*

Where are we going? Are we heading for temptation? Then Christ goes with us to shield us. Are we headed for illness, perhaps even anticipating a visit to the hospital? Then Christ goes with us in all his healing power. Are we going away for the holidays? Then Christ goes with us in the car. No matter what situation we are in — or headed for — the words of Jesus come to us: "Lo, I am with you always."

I am thinking now of Kathryn Koob, who was one of the fifty-two persons who were held as hostages in Iran for more than a year. How was she able to survive? How was she able to maintain her sanity? How did she stand the separation and the loneliness? There is no need to guess at the answers to these questions because she gave us the answers when her captors gave her a chance to speak to her family and friends by way of television. She sang a song: "Be near me, Lord Jesus, I ask Thee to stay close by me forever, and love me, I pray." Kathryn Koob not only survived a very difficult situation, but even said she "felt good" about it, because she knew where God was. He was with her.

Somewhere back in the filing cabinet of my mind, I remember the story of some American soldiers who were about to go overseas during the Second World War. Friends had invited them to a party, and there was a lot of nervous activity and hollow laughter as everyone tried to block out the awful fact that these young soldiers might never return to their homes again. Someone asked the soldiers what they would like as a gift before they departed. There was an awkward silence for a few moments, and then one of the young men said, "We are leaving soon and we may never be back. Is there anyone here who can lead us in singing, 'My Faith Looks Up to Thee"? What a marvelous thing it is that no matter what dreadful circumstances we are called upon to enter, we are able, through faith, to take our God with us!

I have read that there is a beautiful Austrian bridge that has twelve statues of Christ on it. Each one of the statues represents Christ in relation to some particular business or profession. As the herders and shepherds of that area cross the bridge, they pause before the statue of Christ as the Good Shepherd. As the market gardeners and farmers cross the bridge, they stop before Christ the Sower. Fishermen pause before Christ stilling the storm. Those who are doctors and nurses pause before Christ the Healer. By stopping before their particular statue, the persons of each profession are reminded that Christ is their partner and is going with them as they begin a new day's work.

The illustrations could go on and on, but they would only continue to drum home the same point: God's gift of himself, through Jesus Christ our Lord, is the very best gift because his "precious name" and his transforming presence can be taken with us wherever we go.

Finally, God's Gift of Himself Is the Best Christmas Gift Because It Can Be Shared With Others

A gift that has to be kept a secret or hoarded or which causes us to tell others, "Leave that alone, it belongs to me," cannot possibly be the best gift. The very best gifts in life have to be shared. We want to tell others about them. We want to show them to others. We want others to try them.

When the shepherds saw and received the gift of the Christ child, Luke tells us they were simply compelled "to spread the word concerning what had been told them about this child." "Joy to the world; the Lord is come!" and we want to share the good news of the Gift with others. We are so thrilled that we cannot keep our mouths shut about it!

Once there was a Christmas scene on television's "All in the Family" that went like this:

Archie: Stifle, Edith. Let's have a little Silent Night around here for a change . . . I'm the only one around here thinking of the real solemn meaning of Christmas. Which is supposed to be a time of peace and quiet contemplation.

Edith: But I think you're allowed to be jolly, too.

Archie: Sure, Edith, I never said you shouldn't be jolly. Just be jolly with your mouth shut.

Of course, Archie was asking for the impossible — especially at Christmas! We simply cannot be jolly, or joyful, with our mouths shut.

God has given us the best Gift for Christmas — the gift of himself — and we want to share it with everyone. Even John Morley, who was not a Christian, said, "If I believed that Jesus Christ was the Son of God and my Savior, I would never write or talk anything else."

God bless you, and may "the Best Gift" make this the best Christmas you have ever had.

Running Away and Returning

FIRST SUNDAY AFTER CHRISTMAS
Matthew 2:13-15, 19-23

One of the most disappointing experiences of life is the discovery that our heroes are vulnerable. The ones we looked up to for some kind of infallible guidance, the ones who served as our models, we discover, have "feet of clay."

I will never forget the day I discovered that Superman was not so super as I thought he was. This "strange visitor from another planet" was my hero. He was "faster than a speeding bullet, more powerful than a locomotive, and able to leap tall buildings with a single bound." He was able to fly and was often mistaken for a bird or a plane. His eyes had x-ray vision, he could catch bullets in his teeth, and he could change the course of mighty rivers with a single blast of his super breath. I really thought he was invulnerable, didn't you?

Then one day I discovered that there was one thing that could destroy Superman. It was kryptonite. Horrible word! When a piece of this kryptonite, a mineral from his home planet, got near to Superman, it completely weakened him and divested him of all his super powers. If someone, like Lois Lane or Jimmy Olson, did not remove the kryptonite, then Superman would die.

Having survived the discovery of Superman's vulnerability, I was not nearly as distressed, a few years later, to discover that Achilles — considered the bravest, handsomest and swiftest of the army of Agamemnon — was also vulnerable. You may remember his story. His mother, Thetis, dipped his infant body into the river Styx, and that made him invulnerable *except* for that part of his heel by which she had held him. Of course it was predictable from that day that eventually Achilles would die when an enemy's arrow would penetrate his vulnerable heel.

It is disappointing, isn't it, to discover that even the strongest and bravest of men are vulnerable.

Surely our greatest solace is the knowledge that God is invulnerable. Right? Wrong! At least if we take today's Scripture lesson seriously. For Matthew seems to be telling us that Christmas means that even God is vulnerable. By his own choice, to be sure, but vulnerable nonetheless.

Recall this famous passage from Philippians:

Have this mind among yourselves, which is yours in Christ Jesus, who, though he was in the form of God, did not count equality with God a thing to be grasped, but emptied himself, taking the form of a servant, being born in the likeness of men. And being found in human form he humbled himself and became obedient unto death, even death on a cross. (2:5-8)

When God chose to become flesh in the human form of Jesus, he also chose to make himself vulnerable.

What could be more vulnerable than a tiny baby boy in a Bethlehem manger? Do you remember just how fragile a baby is? I held one recently during a baptismal service and was freshly impressed with its delicacy. I thought if I dropped the baby, it would break! What a tremendous risk God took when he chose to reveal himself in the "human form" of the baby Jesus.

Shepherds would rush to greet him. Wise Men would offer him valuable gifts and fall at his feet in worship. It is a powerful scene, but part of the power lies precisely in the apparent weakness, or the vulnerability of the one who was greeted and worshiped.

Matthew addresses himself to this vulnerability in today's Scripture lesson. The lesson divides itself quite naturally into two parts: running away and returning.

First, there is the

Running Away

My copy of the Bible entitles this sub-section of Scripture, "The Flight into Egypt." Cruel Herod the king had been threatened by the birth of Jesus, apparently fearing that Jesus would become a competitor for his own crown. Since that was an intolerable possibility to him, and since he could not be absolutely sure which baby boy was Jesus, he ordered that all the male children in and around Bethlehem who were two-years old or under be killed. Thus it was that an angel of the Lord directed Joseph to take Jesus and Mary and to "flee to Egypt."

Can you imagine it? God on the run! Jesus, the Christ, fleeing for his life! Where is Superman now? Where is the bravest and handsomest and swiftest of all the army of Agamemnon? He is running for his life, to put it bluntly, because Herod is more deadly than kryptonite and more dangerous than the enemy's arrow.

If this scene is shocking for you — and I confess that it is still shocking to me — then hold on, for there is more to come. We can imagine Joseph escaping into Egypt with the *baby* Jesus. But, surely, we think, if Jesus were only a full-grown man, he would not run from Herod. The evidence, however, does not completely support our thought.

There were times, even as an adult, when Jesus ran

away. During the Feast of Dedication in Jerusalem one winter, some people wanted Jesus to tell them "plainly" if he was, indeed, the Christ. When Jesus answered, "I and the Father are one," they took up stones to stone him. We read, "Again they tried to arrest him, but he escaped from their hands." (John 10:39) Notice that word, "again"; apparently Jesus had had to run away on other occasions, too.

There is no getting away from it: Christmas tells us that God chose to make himself vulnerable when he revealed himself in a person who, sometimes, at least, had to run away from people like Herod and the stone-throwers.

Before we go any further, however, we should say this: Please do not make the mistake of thinking that the vulnerability of Christ is a bad thing. It is not! It is a tremendous thing. In fact, it is the greatest thing in the world. For we are saved by a Christ who "took the form of a servant . . . and humbled himself and became obedient unto death, even death on a cross." What men called "the weakness of God" was "the power of God unto salvation." It is a Christ who was willing to risk becoming as vulnerable as we are, who is able to save us from sin by identifying with our human condition and showing us the way back to fellowship with God.

The vulnerability of Christ is a great thing also because it makes it easier for us to admit our own vulnerability. We may like to think that we are super men and women, but we are not. There are powers and people who can hurt us and destroy us. There are times when we need to run away!

You see, running away is not always cowardice as many of us have been taught to believe. Running away, at times, may be part of a very wise strategy. As the old saying goes: "He who runs away lives to fight another day."

There are times, of course, when we cannot run away.

There are times when we must not run away. A man who had given his life in the service of suffering humankind in London was asked by a friend, "Why don't you run away from it all before you are broken by this inhuman burden?" He replied, "I would like to run away. I would like to run away from it all, but a strange Man on a cross won't let me." There are times when running away is cowardice. Jesus did not run away from his betrayers in the Garden of Gethsemane. There are times when we must stand our ground, no matter what the cost.

Nevertheless, there are other times when it is wise to run away. Timing has a lot to do with it. So do our intentions about returning. For after the time of running away, there should always be a time of

Returning

Here is the difference between cowardice and heroism. The coward runs away and stays away. The hero runs away but he always returns at the appropriate time.

I have a biography of *General Douglas MacArthur* that was written by Bob Considine. The picture on the front cover shows the general standing like a boulder, looking off into the distance, with that famous corncob pipe in his mouth. You can almost hear him telling the people of the Philippines, "I came through and I shall return." Ordered to make a strategic withdrawal, his promise to return became the rallying cry for a whole country. MacArthur had to "run away" for a while, but he would "return" — and it was the returning that mattered most.

Jesus ran away into Egypt, but he returned!

All of our running away, as Christians, should be with the ultimate goal of returning.

Why do *we* run away? When I look at my own experience, I find that I usually run away for one of three reasons: I am frightened; I am fatigued; or I am frustrated. Isn't that why you run away, too?

Let us look at fatigue first because that is probably the experience we feel most at this particular time of the year. The Christmas holiday is over for most of us. It has been a very tiring week! The children have been home from school and it has been lovely to have them with us, but their additional activities and demands have overloaded schedules that were already full. We have spent a lot of time visiting with members of the family and friends. In return, we have entertained many visitors to our own homes. There have been seasonal parties at our places of work. We have checked out all the local stores in order to take advantage of their post-holiday sales. It has been fun, but it has also been fatiguing. We are tired and need a break. We need to run away for a while in order to be renewed in body, mind and spirit. We know that we will have to return, eventually, to our normal routines, but for right now, we need a strategic retreat.

Jesus ran away when he got tired. Following the news of John the Baptizer's death, Mark tells us that Jesus said to his disciples:

> *"Come away by yourselves to a lonely place, and rest a while." For many were coming and going and they had no leisure even to eat. And they went away in the boat to a lonely place by themselves. (6:31,31)*

Of course he would return, but for now, he needed to get away for a while and relax.

There were other times, Mark tells us, "After [Jesus] had dismissed the crowds, he went up on the mountain by himself to pray. When evening came, he was there alone." (14:23) Jesus was resting and communing with his heavenly Father in order to find new strength for new tasks in the days that were ahead.

Gautama, the Buddha, was another religious leader who had discovered the value of occasional retreats. He maintained a staggering routine of training monks, directing the affairs of his order, public preaching and private counseling. In order to survive, he developed a pattern of "running away and returning."

He withdrew for six years, then returned for forty-five. But each year was similarly divided: He spent nine months in the world and then retreated to be with his monks during the rainy season. His daily schedule followed the same pattern: His public hours were long, but three times a day he withdrew, that through meditation, he might be restored to the sacred center of his inner being.

Historian Arnold Toynbee says that the "withdraw and return" pattern of Jesus and Buddha is basic to all creativity throughout human history. It is what enables people to stand up under pressure.

I have only recently discovered that even Superman had his Fortress of Solitude to which he flew when he needed to get away for periods of rest, self-examination and renewal.

The point is that we, too, are vulnerable. We become tired. We get worn down and worn out, and we need to run away to a quiet place where we can have long talks with ourselves and with our God. Like MacArthur, "we shall return," and we will be fresher, stronger and livelier persons when we do.

We also run away when we get frustrated. I have a friend who took a summer chemistry course at Salisbury State College (Maryland) this past June and July. It had been twenty years since he had chemistry in high school, and now he was trying to do a whole semester's work of college-level chemistry in five weeks! When I spoke to him one Sunday morning, he had until the next day to read four chapters in his textbook, write up five labs, and memorize thirty formulas. If he had worked non-stop from the time I saw him until the sun rose on Monday, he might have completed his assignments! Yet, when I stopped by the tennis court that afternoon to watch some church members who were playing in a tournament, there was my friend, the chemistry student!

He had gotten so frustrated in his studies that he simply had to run away from them for a while. Do you know what? He went back to his studies two hours later, so refreshed and relaxed after watching a tennis match, that he completed his assignments well ahead of schedule!

There are times when it is wise to run away from frustrating situations. The important thing is that after the time of running away, there is also a time for returning — hopefully with new insight and strength.

Most obvious of all, perhaps, there are times when we run away from things that frighten us. Granted, as a general rule, the best way to destroy our fears is to face them. Nevertheless, there are times when it is the wisest strategy to run away from the Herods and the stone-throwers of this world.

I read about a psychiatrist whose highest priority is his own self-preservation. That is, if a patient comes to him with a problem that he does not feel he can cope with at that particular time, he will refuse to see the patient. At first, I thought that the psychiatrist was being very selfish, but then it dawned upon me that he was simply applying some of his professional insight to himself. He was recognizing his own vulnerability as a person and making responsible allowances for it. He was afraid that he would not be able to maintain his own sanity if he pushed himself beyond his known limits. So he ran away from some appointments — in order that he might return and do the most good for the most people, over the long run.

It doesn't do any good, does it, to deny our own vulnerability if, in the process, we ourselves as well as others, are badly damaged or destroyed?

Christmas tells us that Jesus the Christ is vulnerable, and that is good news, not bad. For we are saved by a Christ who deliberately chose to be vulnerable, and we are given new insights into our own vulnerability.

There is nothing wrong with running away when our running away is part of a deliberate strategy to find new insight and strength through communion with our heavenly Father and through getting in touch with our own higher and better selves.

Jesus ran away.

Superman ran away.

And so do we.

But Jesus returned!

Superman returned!

And so do we!

To Woo and Win a World

SECOND SUNDAY AFTER CHRISTMAS
John 1:1-18

Once upon a time, there was a prince who rode his carriage to town to do some chores for his father. As he was riding through a rather poor section of town, he happened to glance out the window and right into the eyes of a beautiful maiden.

In the days that followed, he returned to that section of town, and once or twice he actually had the good fortune to meet the beautiful maiden. Soon he began to feel that he was in love with her. But now he had a problem. How should he go about winning her hand and making her his bride?

Of course he could order her to the palace and use the pressure of his royal office to force her to marry him. But even a prince would like to feel that the girl who married him did so because she wanted to. He could masquerade as a peasant and try to gain her interest. Then, after he had proposed, he could pull off his "mask" and reveal his true identity. But such a masquerade would be phony, and the prince had too much integrity to attempt that approach.

Finally, another possibility presented itself to his mind. He would discard his kingly robes and move into the neighborhood where the beautiful maiden lived. He would get a job as an ordinary workman, perhaps as a carpenter. He would get acquainted with the people and learn to share their interests and concerns. He would learn to speak their language. In due time, should good fortune be with him, he would introduce himself to the maiden in a very natural and normal way. Should she come to love him, as he had already come to love her, then he would ask for her hand in marriage.

That is what he did. When she did, in fact, come to love him, he told her who he really was.

This story, told a century ago by a Danish theologian named Soren Kierkegaard, is really a parable of Christmas. Indeed, it is an imaginative version of the Christmas story as told in John 1:1-18.

Like the prince, God had fallen in love — not just with a maiden but with a whole world. He longed to win that world to himself, to bring it into a living relationship with him so that he and the world could live happily ever after. But how was he to accomplish his purpose? He could have ordered us to love him, but love that is not voluntarily given is not worth having. In fact, it really isn't love at all. He could have tried a masquerade, but that would have been transparent. The only thing he could do to win us was to meet us on our own level and to woo us. So he came to us on our own terms: "the Word became flesh and dwelt among us, . . ." (John 1:14)

First as a beautiful child, then as a fine young man, he came to meet us. Then as a competent carpenter and a traveling minister he moved among us. When some of us responded to him and returned his love, then he revealed who he was.

If you like big words, you can call it the Incarnation: the love of God "enfleshing" itself in the human form of Jesus, the Christ, in order to woo us and to win us to himself. It is such a big word and such a tremendous concept, though, that it may help us to break it down into smaller and more manageable segments. So I invite you to join me in a consideration of three words that are easier to deal with: identification, involvement and illumination.

Identification

The "Word became flesh," says John. At least that is the way the *Revised Standard Version* of the Bible translates the Greek text. "So the word of God became a human being," says J. B. Phillips' translation. The *New Berkeley Version of the Bible in Modern English* says, "the Word became man." William Barclay is even more direct in his translation: "So the word of God became a person."

God knew that if he was going to woo us and win us, he was going to have to begin by becoming one of us. He was going to have to identify with our human condition, and he did that by becoming a person in the human flesh and form of Jesus.

It may help you to know that at the time of Jesus' birth, there were many people who thought that human flesh was a very wicked thing and the source of much evil. There was even a group of people, known as the Docetists, who were so repulsed by the idea of relating God to human flesh, that they maintained that Jesus only *seemed* to have a body. In fact, they said, Jesus was really a phantom. His body was not a real body; it was only a disembodied spirit in the apparent form of a man. But the writer of John's Gospel would have none of that! When he said that the "Word became flesh," he meant that God did, in truth, reveal himself through a human body just like ours. It completely "blew the minds" of some of the people of that day. It was a completely new thing to say that God loved us so much that he would actually enter into the body of a person and live the life we lived.

I do not say all of this to give you a theological lecture! I say it so you will better see the greatness of the love of a God who longed so much to win us that he identified himself with us!

When we are tempted to belittle the implications of

the Christian faith for the care of our own bodies or for the responsible use of any material thing, we had best beware. For at that point, as Frederick Buechner has suggested, we are attempting to be more "spiritual" than God!

How wise is God! He knew he could not win us unless he identified himself with us through Jesus.

That may be why Dr. Homer Jernigan once told a pastoral care class at Boston University School of Theology, "The most effective form of communication is incarnation."

Several years ago, an atomic scientist was arguing for the value of exchange scholarships between nations. He was not thinking of Christmas, but he gave us a beautiful picture of Christmas when he said, "The best way to send an idea is to wrap it up in a person." You see, that is what God did in the Incarnation: He took the idea of his love and he wrapped it up in the person of Jesus Christ. "The Word became flesh."

This is also our own agenda as Christians: to become so identified with the loving spirit of the God who revealed himself through Jesus, that when people look at us, they will see something of God in us.

I have been reading again *The Autobiography of a Plain Preacher* by Raymond H. Huse. He tells of a little four-year-old girl who lived in one of the parishes he served. One day she was sick in bed and said to her mother, "I wish I could see God." Her mother thought she must want to see the picture of Jesus which hung in her Sunday School room and told her she could see it again when she got well. But the little girl insisted, "I want to see God." Then the mother gave her a little theological lecture on the invisibility of the deity. But with growing impatience, the little girl said, "I want to see the little God with white hair that stands on the platform at church." Of course, she was referring to Huse.

God knew that the only way to win us was to woo us

into loving him. John's Gospel tells us that his method of wooing us was the Incarnation, and this means that the first thing God had to do was to identify with us, through Jesus Christ our Lord.

Involvement

God's identification with us did not take place on a superficial level. We have already hinted at this but it is so important that it must be underscored. The Word that became flesh "dwelt among us." The God who became a human being actually "lived among us." In other words, God got involved with our human situation in a deep and continuing way!

Remember the prince in Kierkegaard's story. He was wise enough to recognize that the only way he could win the hand of the beautiful maiden was to become involved in the kind of life she lived and in her particular neighborhood. That is the kind of involvement that God expressed and continues to express for us through Jesus Christ.

I love the way that Helmut Thielicke makes this point in his book, *Christ and the Meaning of Life.* After stressing the relatedness of the crib and the cross, Thielicke writes, "Jesus Christ did not remain at base headquarters in heaven, receiving reports of the world's suffering from below and shouting a few encouraging words to us from a safe distance. No, he left the headquarters and came down to us in the frontline trenches, right down to where we live and worry . . ., where we contend with our anxieties and the feeling of emptiness and futility, where we sin and suffer guilt, and where we must finally die. There is nothing that he did not endure with us. He understands everything."

I will tell you this: Anyone who loves me so much that he is willing to become *that* involved on my behalf has already won my heart, and he may have my loyalty also!

I could not stand against so great a love, even if I wanted to! Can you?

When the late Dr. Tom Dooley was asked about the success of his Medico program — a program of medical aid to underprivileged foreign countries — he replied, "We actually believe that we can best win the friendship of people only by getting down on the ground and working beside them in . . . a person-to-person program."

Without intending it, Dr. Dooley was really copycatting another person-to-person "program" that God had started twenty centuries earlier in the Incarnation. For on the first Christmas, God had shown his love for us by "getting down on the ground" in the person of Jesus in order to "work beside us" and to help and befriend us.

As we enter into the coming week, we are going to run into some difficult people, and we are going to experience some discouraging and heart-breaking situations. We are going to engage once again in a world that has a lot of problems, both at home and abroad. What a comfort it is to know that the Incarnation means that God loves us so much that he will continue to get involved in our world — even in "the front-line trenches" of our own local neighborhoods — in order to help us and save us and win us back to himself.

What a challenge it is to know that the "other side" of the Incarnation means that we should get involved on behalf of others, just as God has gotten involved on our behalf.

I will never forget the first pastoral call I made, while I was still in the first year of seminary. It was to a woman who was in the hospital for no apparent physical cause. She was heart-broken and desperately lonely. I did not know what to do or to say. I have learned better since then, but in those days I thought I had to do or to say *something.* The best I could manage, under the pressure of the moment, was to say to her, "But Mrs. Snyder, God loves you!" And she said to me, "I don't care if *God* loves me or not; I want my *husband* to love me!"

I don't think I did Mrs. Snyder much good that day, but I sure learned a valuable lesson. It really doesn't do much good to tell a person that God loves him or her, unless we — as husbands, wives, parents, friends, neighbors, pastors, etc. — are willing to wrap that love in our own flesh and to express it in a very practical and helpful way. Our job as Christians is to convince people like Mrs. Snyder that God loves them, by actually demonstrating his love through our own relationship with them. Now, I would say that that job is indeed a challenging one, wouldn't you?

I am glad that Thielicke and others have pointed out the relationship of the crib and the cross. For God's involvement on our behalf, which began at Christmas, continued on to and beyond Good Friday. Thus the famous statement that George MacLeod made about the cross is also appropriate for the Christmas season:

> *I simply argue that the cross be raised again at the center of the marketplace as well as on the steeple of the church. I am recovering the claim that Jesus was not crucified in a cathedral between two candles, but on a cross between two thieves; on the town garbage heap; at a crossroad so cosmopolitan that they had to write his title in Hebrew and in Latin and in Greek . . . at the kind of place where cynics talk smut, and thieves curse, and soldiers gamble. Because that is where he died. And that is what he died about. And that is where churchmen ought to be, and what churchmen should be about.*

Talk about involvement! Nothing but a God-sized love could motivate such involvement as that! So "the Word became flesh and dwelt among us." "The word of God became a person, and took up his abode in our being," in order to identify with us and to save us and to win us to himself.

Illumination

I do not know what you expected to find when you came into the worship service today. Karl Barth, the great theologian, preacher and teacher of preachers, thought he knew when he wrote: "The congregation is waiting for the meaning of life to be illumined by the light of God."

I hope and pray that has happened for you today as we have considered John's version of the Christmas story.

For now we know what the world is like. It is a place, it is a people — like us and others — that God wills to win.

Now we know what God is like, for we have seen him in Jesus, the Christ, our Lord. His life is "the true light that enlightens every man" and shows us what God is like. He is a lover who is out to woo and win us, even as the prince in Kierkegaard's story was out to woo and win his beautiful maiden.

Now we know better who we are and what we are like. For in identifying with us and becoming so involved in our humanity, Jesus has not only shown us what God is like, but he has given us a new sense of personal dignity and worth. He has shown us possibilities that we did not believe existed. He has shown us that we are persons whom God loves. He has shown us that we are persons who are called to share in his Incarnation by demonstrating his love in all our relationships with others.

Truly, the meaning of our lives has been illumined for us by Jesus Christ who is the light and life of God.

So the prince discarded his kingly robes and moved into the neighborhood where the beautiful maiden lived. He got a job as an ordinary workman. He got acquainted with the people and learned to share their concerns and interests. He learned to speak their language. In due time, he introduced himself to the maiden in a very normal and natural way. Fortunately, she came to love him, as he had already come to love her. They were married, and to the best of my knowledge, they lived together happily ever after!

Worship for the Person
Who Has Everything

EPIPHANY OF OUR LORD
Matthew 2:1-12

This is not the sermon I had wanted to preach! I should not tell you that, perhaps, but this honest confession may provide the best way to get into the sermon I am going to preach.

Several years ago, I was fascinated by the concluding phrase in Matthew's famous story of the Wise Men. You will remember that when the Wise Men stopped in Jerusalem, on their way to find the Christ child, Herod summoned them into a secret meeting. He told them, "When you have found (the child) bring me word that I too may come and worship him." Well, the Wise Men went on about their business: They found the child, worshiped him, and gave him gifts. Then we read, "And being warned in a dream not to return to Herod, they departed to their own country by another way."

I fell in love with that phrase: "they departed . . . by another way." The *Good News Bible* says that they departed "by another road."

I thought: If I ever get a chance to write a sermon on the Wise Men, I will build it around that phrase. I will call it, "Home — By Another Road," and I will picture the Wise Men coming to Jesus as persons who are weak and wretched and hopeless. Then, as a result of their worship, I will send them "Home — By Another Road," as persons who were now strong and beautiful and hopeful.

Then lo and behold, I got the chance to write such a sermon. But it wouldn't work! I tried to make it work, but it refused. I pushed it, I kicked it, I shoved it and tried every cute manipulation in the book, and it still wouldn't work! I simply couldn't understand what was wrong. Then, finally, after a week or more of pure frustration, it dawned on me why my beautiful sermon idea would not work.

It wouldn't work because it was wrong in its premise. The Wise Men were not weak; they were strong. They were not wretched; they were beautiful. They were not hopeless; they were hopeful. And here was the bombshell — the Wise Men were all of those good things *before* they even met Christ or had the chance to worship him! Those fellows were better off when they went *into* the worship service than many of us are when we *leave* the worship service.

So here we are in *this* sermon, talking about "Worship for the Person Who Has Everything."

The Wise Men were leaders of their day. They were the scientists, men who were skilled in philosophy, medicine and astrology. They were wealthy enough to take a two-year sabbatical, buy extravagant gifts, and go running off across a world to pay homage to a newborn king. They were healthy-minded men and had a very reverent attitude toward life.

What more could they have wanted. They were persons who already had everything! Hear this — for here is the value of this particular sermon — the Wise Men were exactly like a lot of people in the world and in this country and in this town and in this congregation today. They have everything: They hold responsible positions of leadership; they are affluent; they have beautiful houses and lovely families; they are strong and healthy-minded; they are basically reverent in their attitudes toward life; and they are rightly respected in the community.

The Need to Worship

Yet, if we take the experience of the Wise Men seriously, even these people who have everything need to worship.

It is a shame that we have tended to reserve worship exclusively for those persons who are weak and mean and miserable: for those who don't have anything. Of course, worship is for those persons, too, but in its concentration on those who are "down-and-out," the church has often forgotten to be concerned about those who are "up-and-out."

In fact, some preachers, and even some hymn writers, have focused so much on the idea of the miserable sinner, that some people who have a higher image of themselves are offended. I will never forget the time when, as just a young preacher, I was invited to preach in a big suburban church whose members were very affluent and sophisticated. As is customary, I had mailed my sermon theme and hymn numbers to the church office well ahead of time. One of the hymns, which fit the theme of the day, was "Amazing Grace." When I arrived at the church on the morning I was to preach, I was met by the organist-choirmaster, who said to me, "We don't sing that hymn in this congregation. Now I have picked out some more acceptable hymns which have the same theme, and we will sing any one of those that you want." I learned later that what offended that congregation — or at least the organist — was the hymn's reference to "a wretch like me!"

My first response was to be intimidated by the organist, for I was young. Later, my response turned to anger. Now, many years later, I think I have much more sympathy for the organist's point of view.

The church has not been wrong, of course, in offering God's "Amazing Grace" to "the wretches" of the world, but the church may not have spent enough time in offering God's "Amazing Grace" to those who are already strong — and in doing so in images and language that are meaningful to them.

For even those who have everything, like the Wise Men, also need to worship. The fact of the matter is that "things," no matter how many of them you have, are not an adequate basis for a meaningful life. No matter how much a person has to live *on*, he/she also needs something to live *for*.

James Barrie's little play, entitled "The Will," illustrates this fact.

The play opens with the happy newlyweds, Mr. and Mrs. Philip Ross, in the office of a lawyer drawing up a will. Philip is so in love with his wife that he wants to make the will only one sentence long and leave everything to her. But she feels that their money should be shared with Philip's cousins and a convalescent home. The lawyer likes their attitude and says, "You are a ridiculous couple. But don't change."

Twenty years pass, and Philip and his wife return to the lawyer's office to make up a new will. By now the Rosses have become very rich, and Mrs. Ross does not want Philip to do anything foolish, like including his cousins in the new will. They fight bitterly over how the money should be disposed of. The convalescent home is left out altogether. Both Philip and his wife refer to the money as "my money."

Another twenty-five years pass, and Philip, now sixty-five, comes back to the lawyer's office. His wife is dead. His children have turned out poorly. He wants to revise his will. This time he leaves nothing to his relatives. He doesn't think his children deserve to be remembered. He doesn't want to share his money with any good cause.

He starts to dictate his new will to the lawyer. "I leave it — I leave it — my God, I don't know what to do with it!" Finally, he shouts in anger, "Here are the names of half a dozen men I fought to get my money. I beat them. Leave it to them, with my curses."

Now the Rosses were people who had everything — at least in the eyes of the world. But they didn't have a purpose or a vision of life that was big enough to give meaning to their possessions. There was no cause that was big enough to give a sense of direction to their first positive impulses.

To put it in a nutshell: They had everything — almost! But they didn't have a God to whom they could dedicate themselves and their possessions. They didn't have a Lord who was big enough to channel their basic goodness and strength into a creative and healthy usefulness. So they turned sour. That is usually what happens when the person who has everything to live *on* doesn't have Anyone to live *for.*

So the Wise Men, at least, felt the need to worship, and they set off across a whole world to find a King, a Christ, who could give a meaning and a purpose to their lives.

Worship as Gratitude

When the Wise Men saw the star stop over the place where Christ was, they were filled with great joy. "And going into the house they saw the child . . ., and they fell down and worshiped him. Then, opening their treasures, they offered him gifts, gold and frankincense and myrrh."

Gratitude is the predominant note of worship for the person who has everything. The emphasis is on giving rather than on getting. Where did the strong person get his strength? From God. Where did the responsible leader get her ability? From God. Where do wise people get their wisdom? From God. Who is the source of meaning and purpose in life? It is the God who revealed himself to us in Jesus Christ our Lord.

Worship is saying "Thank you" to God!

It is a tragedy that so many of us have let ourselves fall into the mistaken notion that the basic element in worship is getting something from God. We "go to worship" in order to get health or happiness or personal peace or financial success or some material possession. Our request to God is the same that the Prodigal Son made to his father: "Give me . . ."

One of the problems is that the "getting" attitude leads to the "keeping" attitude, and that is contrary to everything that the Christian faith, at its best, represents.

I am reminded of the wealthy executive who was solicited by a neighbor for a gift to the United Fund. The executive said that he had many obligations.

For example, did the solicitor know that his father's farm was about to be foreclosed and that his mother needed an operation?

"No."

Did the solicitor know that his brother was badly disfigured in an automobile accident and needed plastic surgery?

"No."

Did the solicitor know his brother-in-law was going to prison unless he made up a shortage in his accounts by next Tuesday, and if he did go to prison, his sister said she would shoot herself and the children?

"No," said the solicitor, nervously backing toward the door. He had not known all those things.

"Well," said the executive, "if I'm not giving any of them a dime — and I am not — why should I contribute to the United Fund?"

What a positive contribution that wealthy executive could have made to the lives of many people, if only he had seen God as the source of his material blessings and had thanked God for them and had shared them with others who were less fortunate than he!

When the Wise Men offered their gifts — their very valuable gifts — to the Christ child, they were affirming that gratitude is the predominant theme in the worship of those who have everything.

Akira Sueno travels a lot, and it is his belief that a person should be able to express the basic feeling of gratitude in the local language of whatever country he happens to be in. Therefore, the first thing he does whenever he visits a new country is to learn to say "thank you" in that local language.

So, in America he says "Thank you," in Germany he says "Danke," in Finland he says "Kiitos," in Sweden he says "Tak," in France he says "Merci," in Italy he says "Grazie," in Israel he says "Todaraka," and in India he says "Dyanyabad."

But no problem! God understands all languages, and he is pleased when we say "Thank you" to him for all that we have and are. He is especially thankful when our worship becomes a means of expressing our gratitude for Jesus Christ, our Lord.

The person who has everything really doesn't have everything until he gains a thankful heart. People who have everything still need to worship, and the predominant note of their worship is gratitude.

Benefits of Worship

There are benefits, of course, even for those who have everything. But the benefits are really a serendipity. That is, they are "valuable or agreeable things that were not sought for." They are the byproducts of a worship that says "Thank you" to God, without expecting to receive anything else in return. But, lo and behold, it seems that God decides to give the most valuable gifts to

62

those who were not even seeking them!

So the Wise Men — those ancient prototypes of all those modern people who already have everything — worshiped Christ and gave him gifts, and the Almighty God gave them even greater gifts in return.

God gave them a larger vision of the Kingship, the Lordship, of Jesus Christ. They had come to worship "the King of the Jews" and had even told that much to Herod. Now, their worship had revealed to them that Jesus Christ was their King also. The "King of the Jews" was also the King of the Gentiles, and everybody else's king too, for that matter!

Worship, at its best, always gives us a larger vision of the Lordship of Jesus Christ. This is one of the great themes of the church season of Epiphany which "begins" today. The God who revealed himself in Jesus Christ is the Lord of all people, everywhere — irrespective of race, creed, color, sex, income, or anything else.

G. Ray Jordan, who used to be the Teacher of Preaching at Emory University's Candler School of Theology in Atlanta, Georgia, told of a dramatic incident in the life of Rabbi Cohen of Texas. The Jewish leader was not getting much sleep because he was trying to figure out a way to help a certain refugee. Finally, he decided to borrow the money to go to Washington in order to speak to the Department of Labor on the refugee's behalf.

Officials at the Department told Cohen that it was a clear cut case of illegal entry and referred him to his congressman.

The congressman could not help him but did agree to get him an appointment with President Taft. Taft was kind and friendly to the Rabbi but told him that the Department of Labor had rendered its decision and there was nothing that he could do about it.

Realizing that he was defeated, Rabbi Cohen was sick at heart, as well as physically exhausted. He could not hide his sadness as he thanked the President for seeing him and stood up to leave.

"I'm sorry this had to happen to you, Rabbi Cohen," said President Taft. "But allow me to say that I certainly admire the way you Jewish people help each other out — traveling all the way up here from Galveston, Texas, when a member of your faith is in trouble."

"Member of my faith! This man is not a Jew," Rabbi Cohen exclaimed. "He's a Greek Catholic."

Taft's face registered his surprise. "You mean to say, you traveled all the way up here at your own expense to help out a Greek Catholic!"

Cohen replied: "He's in trouble; they are going to deport him on the next ship, and he'll face a firing squad when he gets back to Russia. He's a human being, Mr. President; a human life is at stake. That's the way I see it."

The President was so impressed with Cohen's magnanimous spirit that he "pulled the strings" to have the refugee released to Cohen's personal custody.

Such largeness of spirit is one of the benefits of genuine worship, and it is the beginning of true wisdom. Under God, there is an essential kinship among people. It transcends race, nation, and every kind of group loyalty.

Even people who already have every *thing* would benefit from such a largeness of spirit.

Then, the Wise Men also benefited from their worship in another way.

The strength and resources they already enjoyed were redirected in a more positive and healthy direction. It would not be too much to say, I think, that they made a personal commitment of themselves and their resources to Jesus Christ.

On their way to Bethlehem, they were not hesitant to "farm out" their services to King Herod. If Herod wanted them to do something for him, they would do it! If Herod wanted to hire them part-time to scout out the whereabouts of the Christ child and then report back to him, that was quite all right!

But then they met the Christ and they worshiped him and something happened to them. They didn't want anything to do with King Herod. Their loyalty, now, was to King Jesus, not Herod. So, to avoid Herod altogether, "they departed to their own country by another way." "They returned to their country by another road."

I am sure that that statement is a literal statement of an actual fact. I am just as sure that the statement also reflects what happened *inside* of the Wise Men. They went home by a different road because they were different people. They were different people because they had met and worshiped Jesus the Christ, and Christ had given them a larger vision of the Kingdom of God, and Christ had redirected their strength and loyalty into the service of his own cause.

The Wise Men would never be the same again! We will never be the same again, either. For the people who *thought* they had everything really didn't! They worshiped and expressed their gratitude to the God who came in Jesus Christ, and that God gave himself to them. Then the people who only *thought* they had everything, *really did* have everything. For they had Christ, or it would be better to say, he had them!

A final, brief suggestion — out of respect to an old sermon that never got preached — except in the introduction of this sermon!

I suggest that you actually return to your homes today "by another road." If you came to worship today by way of the main streets, then return to your homes by the side streets. If you came to the worship service the short way, traveling from the west, then return to your homes the long way, traveling from the east. You get the idea! Go home by roads and streets that are different from those that brought you here.

Let the fact that you are returning home "by another

road" also represent the fact that something great has happened in this worship hour today — and as a result, you are not the same persons as when you came!

With Christ, you are, finally, the people who have Everything!

"That's My Son!"

BAPTISM OF OUR LORD
FIRST SUNDAY AFTER EPIPHANY
Matthew 3:13-17

The Dover District of the Peninsula Conference, of which I am a part, held its last Ministers and Mates Christmas party at Whatcoat United Methodist Church in Camden, Delaware. The leader of the program that night was the gifted minister of music from Avenue Church in Milford, Delaware. At one point, the leader invited the children to join him at the front of the room to sing some Christmas carols. My own beautiful son, John Thomas, who is now seven-and-a-half years of age, was one of the children who responded. The leader asked some of the children, including John Thomas, to sing short solo parts. It was an exciting and entertaining time. When John Thomas had finished singing, I was so proud I thought I would burst. Spontaneously, without any conscious attempt to show off, I found I was standing on my feet and proudly announcing to everyone in the room — to everyone in the world, for that matter: "That's my boy! That's my son!"

I take the time to tell you this personal story because I think that God said something like that at the Baptism of his Son.

You remember the story of that Baptism as recorded in Matthew 3:13-17. Jesus had come down to the Jordan River to be baptized by John. John was hesitant to perform the Baptism, telling Jesus, in effect, "You have got this thing backwards. You ought to be baptizing me." And Jesus replied, "Let it be this way for now." Following the Baptism, as Jesus came up from the water, Matthew says, "the heavens were opened" and the voice of God announced to the whole world, "This is my beloved Son, with whom I am well pleased." In other words, God looked down on Jesus, and he said to all who would listen: "That's my boy! That is *my* son!"

It is important to Matthew that God's announcement was made to everyone who was present at the Baptism. According to Mark's Gospel, God's voice was directed exclusively to Jesus (1:11). But Matthew wants to make it quite clear that the Baptism is an epiphany; that is, God is announcing to the whole church — indeed, to the whole world — the true identity of Jesus. According to Matthew, God seems to be "show-casing" Jesus, putting him on display, so to speak, and saying to us: Look at Jesus — he is my Son — he is my Servant.

Son

"People, look at Jesus," says God. "This is my beloved Son, with whom I am well pleased."

The August 16, 1982, issue of **People** magazine reports another baptism and another proud father. His Royal Highness Prince William Arthur Philip Louis of Wales was baptized in the Music Room of Buckingham Palace by Dr. Robert Runcie, the Archbishop of Canterbury. It is reported that the prince emitted "three little squeaks" as Archbishop Runcie poured the baptismal water over his head. His mother, Diana, blushed at each squeal. Prince Charles gallantly wiped dribbles from his son's chin, and Queen Elizabeth later joked that her grandson showed stage presence. The Archbishop admonished the baby prince's parents and godparents "to bring up this child to fight against evil and follow Christ."

It is said that as Prince Charles goes about his daily duties, "he can't stop talking about the baby." I take that to mean that Charles uses every possible opportunity to mention Prince William and to announce to the whole world: "That's my boy! That is *my* son!"

Surely God must smile at a parent's pride in a child, for he also expressed his pride at the baptism of his own Son.

No wonder that God was proud of Jesus, for there was much of the Father in the life of the Son. Comedienne Gilda Radner, of television fame, was very close to her father, a Detroit businessman who died when she was a teenager. They loved to attend touring-company productions of Broadway shows. "My dad was in real estate and investments," Miss Radner says, "but he loved show biz. He loved to sing, and he couldn't carry a tray of food to the table without tripping to make us kids laugh and make my mother nervous. As I perform now, *I feel that some part of my father is alive in me,* back doing what he always wanted to do." (Italics mine)

It is putting it mildly to say that some part of God was alive in Jesus; through him, God was accomplishing what he always wanted to do.

Perhaps the characteristic of Jesus' life that stands out more clearly than any other is his submission to the will of God. Even as a boy of twelve, he put "his Father's house" and "his Father's business" above everything else. (See Luke 2:41-52). Now he was submitting to the baptism by John, not because he had sinned, but because he believed it was the will of God for his life.

"Let it be so now; for thus it is fitting for us to fulfill all righteousness," he said to John. Such submission to the will of God would continue to characterize the life of Christ until that final moment on the cross when he would say, "Father, into Your hands I commit my spirit."

It is not hard to understand why God was proud of

Jesus and thus said to the whole world: "That is my Son; I am very pleased with him!"

Servant

"People, look at Jesus again," says God. "This is also my beloved Servant, with whom I am well pleased."

I must admit that I probably have an advantage over you at this point, for I have had the opportunity to study the background and the context of our Scripture lesson, Matthew 3:13-17. That study reveals that the voice of God that spoke to Jesus at his baptism spoke in language that echoed two Old Testament passages: Psalm 2:7 and Isaiah 42:1. For example, "This is my beloved Son" echoes Psalm 2:7 which is part of a passage that describes the coming Messiah. "With whom I am well pleased" echoes Isaiah 42:1 which is part of a description of the suffering servant. Therefore, it is a legitimate conclusion that, in echoing these Old Testament passages, Matthew is declaring to the church the true identity of Jesus: not only is he God's Son, but he is also God's chosen servant. This is a major theme of Epiphany, by the way, and explains why we are looking at Matthew 3:13-17 on this particular Sunday.

Whether or not the Old Testament passages we have just mentioned originally referred to Jesus is a theological question we do not need to consider in this sermon. But it does seem clear that Jesus himself eventually came to interpret his life in terms of these passages.

The highest priority of our Lord was always service — service to God through service to the real needs of people. You may remember the time that James and John, the ambitious sons of Zebedee, went to Jesus and asked him for the privilege of being seated in the special places of honor. After telling James and John that they really didn't recognize what they were asking for, and in any case, they wanted something that only God could give, Jesus went on to say, "Whoever would be great among you must be your servant, and whoever would be first among you must be slave of all. For the Son of man also came not to be served but to serve, and to give his life as a ransom for many." (Mark 10:43-45)

I like the way the King James Version of the Bible translates part of this statement of Jesus: "Whosoever will be great among you, shall be your minister . . . For even the Son of man came not to be ministered unto, but to minister, and to give his life a ransom for many."

You see, genuine *service* and genuine *ministry* are the same thing! At his baptism, God confirmed the call of Jesus to ministry. At our own baptisms, God also calls us into the general ministry of service to others. We may or may not go on into the ordained ministry. I, personally, chose that course — or better, felt chosen by it. But every Christian is a minister — by virtue of his or her Christian baptism.

It is a ministry, it is a service, that often requires us to pay a high price, just as our Lord did. You will remember that the image from Isaiah 42:1 was that of a *suffering* servant.

I think of Jackie Robinson and the real service he provided to millions of people — players and fans alike — when he broke a long standing barrier and opened the big leagues to black athletes. As Branch Rickey, owner of the Brooklyn Dodgers, prepared Robinson to sign a contract, he wondered if the young player would be equal to the challenge. Would Robinson be able to stay out of fights, both on and off the field? Could he behave in such a way that he would neither arouse black fans nor openly antagonize white fans? Obviously, Robinson was going to need to be more than just a great player of baseball.

One day, Rickey called Robinson into his office and showed him a copy of Giovanni Papini's book, *The Life of Christ.* Then he quoted these words: "Ye have heard that it hath been said, An eye for an eye, and a tooth for a tooth; But I say unto you, that ye resist not evil: But whosoever shall smite thee on the right cheek, turn to him the other also."

"Now," Rickey said softly to Robinson, "can you do it? You will have to promise that for the first three years in baseball, you will turn your other cheek. I know you are naturally combative. But for three years — three years — you will have to do it the only way it can be done. Three years — can you do it?" Robinson was a devout Christian, but he was going to pay a high price — both for himself and as a service to generations of athletes who would walk the path that he had opened.

When God looked down on Jesus at his baptism, he said, "This is my beloved Son (my Servant), with whom I am well pleased." I believe that when God looked down on Jackie Robinson, he said, "This is my son, too, and I am also very pleased at the way he is serving me."

Real service to real needs does not come cheaply, but we do it gladly and out of a deep sense of appreciation to Jesus Christ who first ministered to us.

Dr. Theodore Parker Ferris, one of my personal heroes in the ministry, told of a traveler out in Africa who was watching a nun dressing the wounds of a leper. The wounds were gruesome and repulsive. As he watched her, the traveler said, "I wouldn't do that for ten thousand dollars." She looked up at him and said, "I wouldn't either." She was not doing it for ten thousand dollars — or for all the money in the world. She was doing it for love — out of gratitude to the One who had loved her and given himself for her. She was doing it out of love for the Christ who said, "as you did it to one of the least of these my brethren, you did it to me." (Matthew 25:40)

Well, we have come a long way from that Christmas party where I was so proud of John Thomas and announced to a whole room full of people, "That's my boy! That's my son!" That was a great day in my life.

It was also a great day when God looked down on Jesus at his Baptism and announced to a whole world, "That is my Son (and my Servant), with whom I am well pleased."

It is also a great day — perhaps the greatest day of all — when God looks down on us and says, "You are my children too, and I am also very pleased at the way *you* are serving me!"

So may it be for us all!

What You Need Is What You See

SECOND SUNDAY AFTER EPIPHANY
John 1:29-41

What we see is determined to a great extent by what we need.

This truth has been illustrated recently in my own experience. The time has come for me to buy a car. I need one. My beloved Capri which has faithfully transported me through three pastoral assignments is ready to be retired (and that is not intended as a pun). I need a new car. Before my need became apparent, I hardly even noticed other cars. They were just so many boxes moving along the highways on four wheels. But now that I need a car, I see cars everywhere I look.

I even talk to myself: There goes a Ford Escort. My, that is a pretty color. Seventy-five hundred dollars, with automatic transmission and air conditioning. There goes a Chevrolet Cavalier. Nice styling. One owner said he got forty miles per gallon of gas. That would be nice. Eighty-five hundred dollars, equipped the way I would like it — and so it goes with every passing car. I am very car conscious these days; what I need determines what I see.

Now — believe it or not — what I have just said about the car situation is relevant to today's Scripture lesson. John 1:29-41 gives us a picture of a many-faceted Jesus. The number of names that this passage uses for Jesus is impressive, and names, as they are used in Scripture, are always significant and treated with great care. Also, John 1:29-41 shows us three persons or groups of persons who respond to Jesus in different ways. The nature of their response seems to be defined by the particular name they assign to Jesus.

John seems to be saying that different people see Jesus differently, usually on the basis of their own needs or their perception of the needs of others. In other words, what we need from Jesus tends to be what we see in Jesus.

The Lamb of God

The first person we meet in the Scripture lesson is John the Baptizer. Everyone knows that he was quite aware of the reality of sin and of the need for repentance. That was his favorite theme. It completely dominated his thinking. He preached on that theme whenever he got the chance.

Whether John saw himself as a sinner is not clear, but he certainly saw the world as being populated with sinful people. Their greatest need was for someone who would take away their sin.

Therefore, we are not surprised that when John saw Jesus walking toward him, he said, "Behold, the Lamb of God, who takes away the sin of the world." The image of "the Lamb of God" would have had rich meaning for John. He had "grown up" on the Old Testament which used the sacrificial lamb as a symbol of one who by his own suffering and sacrifice would redeem the people. That "one," John now believe was Jesus; *he* was the Lamb of God.

I overheard an interesting conversation the other day. Two attractive young mothers were discussing their children's Atari video games. That led to a discussion of television and movies in general. "I really like 'Star Trek,' " said one of the mothers. "It had so many theological implications." "I agree," said the other mother." My son and I recently saw the movie 'Star Trek

II,' and we were so disappointed when Dr. Spock died. He gave himself as a sacrificial lamb, you know, in order to save the other members of the Starship Enterprise." Frankly, I was surprised to hear two very modern and sophisticated young women talking with such ease about a Christ-figure who sacrificed his own life in order to save the lives of others.

If we are aware of our own sinfulness and the sinfulness of others — especially if we have experienced God's forgiving love through Jesus Christ — we tend to look at Jesus and to say with John, "Behold, the Lamb of God, who takes away the sin of the world."

Nothing is more redemptive or inspiring than a person who gives himself on behalf of another. As Jesus said, "Greater love has no man than this, that a man lay down his life for his friends." In *The Grandeur and Misery of Man*, David E. Roberts tells of a conversation that was overheard by Henri Barbusse during the war. The scene was a dugout that was filled with wounded men. One of the men knew he was dying, and he said to another: "Listen, Dominique, you've led a bad life. There are no convictions against me. There's nothing in the books against my name. Take my name. Take my life. I give it to you. Straight off, you've no more convictions. Take it. It's there in my pocketbook. Go on, take it, and hand yours over to me — so that I can carry all your crimes away."

That is also what God says to the human race through the sacrifice of Jesus Christ: "Take my life. I give it to you . . . And hand your life over to me, so that I can carry all your sins away (and give you new life)."

The misery of humans is their sinfulness; their grandeur is the new and abundantly meaningful life that they receive through Jesus, "the Lamb of God, who takes away the sin of the world."

When we need to be saved from sin, then we see Jesus as "the Lamb of God."

Teacher

The second persons we see are "two disciples" who heard John talking about Jesus. They became interested in Jesus and followed him.

When Jesus turned and asked the disciples, "What do you seek?" they addressed him as "Rabbi" (which means Teacher) and replied, "Where are you staying?" It seems clear that they wanted more than a passing conversation with Jesus. They wanted to make a pot of coffee, sit down with him for a while, put their feet up on the desk, and ask him some questions at a leisurely pace.

The particular need of these two disciples, at this particular point in their lives, was to find some answers to their questions. Therefore, when they looked at Jesus, they saw him as the great Rabbi or Teacher.

We must beware of pushing everybody into the same boat — especially if they are headed toward different objectives or destinations. One person may be aware of his sin and, therefore, need to experience Jesus as the Lamb of God. But another person may be aware of his confusion and need to experience Jesus as Teacher.

I have an uneasy feeling that we have not given sufficient attention to Jesus as a great Teacher. We have been so concerned to stress that he is *more* than a teacher, that we may have made him less than a teacher. That is, we have been so concerned to stress that Jesus is Savior and Lord, that we have tended to overlook his contribution as a teacher.

There is also the fact that teachers, and education in general, are not held in the highest esteem these days. D. C. Macintosh tells of the time he crossed the Canadian border into the United States. The American immigration official asked him the usual questions about his citizenship and residence and whether he had employment in the States. When Macintosh told him that the contract for the employment had been made while he was still in Canada, the official told him that he could not enter the United States because he was violating the Alien Labor Law. After a spirited exchange in the conversation, the official glared at Macintosh and said, "What are you going to do?" Macintosh answered that he was going to be a professor at Yale University. "Oh, well!" said the official, "if you are going to be a professor, that's all right. I thought you said you were going to work!"

Jesus was a great professor — a great Teacher — and he worked at it. His parables are masterpieces. His insight into questions — and questioners! — was unequaled. His answers were nothing short of brilliant. Therefore, when the two disciples came to Jesus with their questions, we can be sure that he met their need. We do not know what questions they asked, but they were probably the same kind of questions that we ask.

In response to the questions about God, Jesus said, "He that hath seen me hath seen the Father."

Concerning human nature, he told that great story of "The Prodigal Son."

When asked about prayer, he replied, "When you pray, say, Our Father . . ."

In response to questions about our priorities, he said, "Seek first the Kingdom of God and his righteousness, and all these things shall be yours as well."

Concerning our relationships, he told of a "good Samaritan" who befriended a person in need and then he told us to "go and do likewise."

When asked about the meaning of religion, Jesus said, "Follow me."

When responding to questions about life after death , he taught us, "I am the resurrection and the life; he who believes in me, though he die, yet shall he live . . ."

If our need is to find answers to the really big questions of life, then we look at Jesus and we see him as the world's finest Teacher.

Christ

When Andrew stood off by himself and looked at Jesus, he knew that he had found "the Messiah (which means Christ)." Bless his heart; it seems that Andrew always had the need to be helping others and serving their deepest needs. Practically every time you see him, he is always introducing others — like his brother, Simon Peter — to Jesus.

Andrew needed someone who was worthy of his kind of deep and loyal commitment. Therefore, when he looked at Jesus, he saw the Messiah or the Christ.

It is significant that Andrew would have seen the Messiah through the Old Testament imagery of the Messiah as God's anointed King. Andrew needed someone who was worthy of his service, a King if you will. Therefore, he gave himself to the service of Christ and his Kingdom. Of course, we have the same need to serve our Lord and to give ourselves to his cause.

One of the biggest problems that many people have today is that they never find a truly constructive cause that is big enough to inspire their personal devotion and service. So they spend their tremendous talents in the pursuit of trivial goals. Thus a man with the mathematical potential of an Einstein throws it all down the tubes as he applies his genius to figuring out the "odds" on certain athletic contests or trying to beat the dealers in a gambling casino. Or a woman who has fantastic potential as a teacher sets it all aside in order to give herself to a less worthy — but far more lucrative — position. We need more people who will not stop until they find a cause — a Christian cause — that is big enough to match their talents! Would to God that such people would look to Jesus in their need — as Andrew did — and see in him the Christ who is worthy to receive the very best that they have to offer.

I like the story of the children who were singing the

song, "Praise Him, Praise Him, All Ye Little Children." They sang the verses with great fervor: "Praise Him — Love Him — Serve Him." Suddenly, a church school teacher appeared in the room and announced that hot chocolate and cookies were being served in the kitchen. As the children hurried off in the direction of the kitchen, one little boy tugged at the coat of the song leader and protested: "We forgot to crown him." So all of the children paraded back and sang the final verse of the song: "Crown Him, Crown Him, All ye little children."

All too many times, we have made the same mistake as the children. We have praised the Lord for all the good things he has done for us. We have loved the Lord because he has ministered to our need. We have served the Lord in various ways as we have allowed him to use our brains and hands to do his work. But — and here is the sad part — we have not always taken the time to crown him as the Lord and King — the ruler — of all of life.

When you stop to think about it, however, perhaps our service to the Lord is in itself the most effective way that we can crown him as the Christ and the King — the ruler of every aspect and dimension of our lives.

If our need is to serve, then may we have the insight of Andrew to see Jesus as the Christ, the one who is worthy of receiving our service.

You may have heard the story of the three blind men and the elephant. The men had never experienced an elephant before, and then one day there were asked to touch an elephant and to describe what it was like. The first man touched the elephant's trunk and reported that an elephant is like a large hose. The second man touched the elephant's leg and reported that an elephant is like a tree. The third man touched the elephant's side and reported that an elephant is like a wall. Obviously, it was the same elephant, but each man described it in terms of his personal experience with one part of that huge animal.

John the Baptizer, the two disciples, and Andrew all looked at the same Jesus. John saw Jesus as the Lamb of God who takes away the sins of the world. The two disciples saw Jesus as the Teacher who answers the really big questions in life. Andrew saw Jesus as Christ the King who is worthy to receive the very best we have to offer in terms of devotion and service. In every case, it is the same Jesus, but each person described him in terms of his own personal experience and need.

Jesus is a many-faceted Lord. There is no need of ours that he cannot meet.

What we need in our lives is what we see in him.

Jesus Did Not Settle Down

THIRD SUNDAY AFTER EPIPHANY
Matthew 4:12-23

One of the best things about the Bible is that it was translated into several different versions. You can read a passage in one version of the Bible and it makes no impression at all. Your brain simply sighs "ho-hum." Then you can read the same passage in another version of the Bible and the slightly different phrasing of the same truth seems to have magic in it. Your brain shouts "aha!" and your mind snaps to quick attention. Something great is there and you had missed it.

That is what happened to me when I read Matthew 4:12-23 — same old stuff expressed in the same old way. It was great because it was biblical, but it wasn't particularly exciting. Then I read the passage in *Good News for Modern Man* and one of the phrases leaped off the page and cried out, "Preach on me; preach on me!" The phrase was, "He did not settle down . . ." Isn't that tremendous? Jesus did not settle down.

Jesus was standing on the threshold of his public ministry. He had good news to share. Indeed, he *was* good news. He was going to tell and show the people that God was love. He was going to invite the people into the Kingdom of heaven and tell them which "turns" to take to get there. In his own presence, the Kingdom was already near to the people. Jesus was not going to settle down until everyone everywhere had heard the good news communicated in every possible way.

You can feel the sense of movement oozing through the words of Matthew 4:12-23. Jesus was off and running with the good news, and he would not — he could not — settle down.

Place

Jesus did not settle down in one place. Specifically, we read, "He did not settle down in Nazareth, but went and lived in Capernaum . . ." If I remember church history correctly — and that is not my "strong suit" — Capernaum is now a pile of ruins, but in the days of Jesus, it was a bustling center of commerce. It was a good place to launch a public ministry. But our main concern right now is not that Jesus went *to* Capernaum, but that he *went away from Nazareth.*

It would have been so easy for Jesus to settle down in Nazareth. That was his home town. He knew the people there and they knew him. He knew all the familiar landmarks there and all the local customs. He knew the best places to shop and the best people to call on when he needed help. It would have been so comfortable for Jesus to settle down in Nazareth.

To be perfectly honest, if I were not part of a denomination that practices an itinerant ministry, I probably would have settled down in my home town. But the United Methodist Church, following the wise custom of its founder John Wesley, has said that there is value in a minister moving to a different place from time to time. The rationale for such movement is both practical and theological. Practically, if a minister stays in one place too long, there is a tendency for him to start building his own kingdom, instead of concentrating on "bringing in" the Kingdom of God. Theologically, any given place will probably come closer to fulfilling its God-given mission if it is served by a variety of ministers with different gifts and graces, over a period of time.

In any case, recognizing that there are exceptions to any rule, it is probably best if ministers today follow the example of Jesus and refuse to settle down in one place for too long. There is a whole world out there that needs to hear the good news, and we need to keep moving until all have heard and had a chance to respond.

Unfortunately, too much of our movement in the church is nothing more than verbal. I like the story of the public meeting that had gone on for several hours. Everyone was bored nearly to death, fighting to stay awake and hardly aware of what was being said. Someone handed a note to the chairman, which said, "Someone has parked a minibus in front of a fire hydrant. Will someone please move the minibus?" The chairman looked at the note and then read it to the whole group, ending, of course, with the question, "Will someone please move the minibus?" Immediately, a young man in the back of the room stood up and said, "Mister chairman, I move the minibus." Then a young lady stood up and said, "Mister chairman, I second the motion." And the chairman, rapping the table with his gavel, said with great gusto: "Now that the minibus has been moved, let's get on to some other business!"

As we said, too much of the church's movement is merely verbal. We settle down in the lounge of the church building in air-conditioned comfort, and we talk about the mission of the church. We talk and we talk and we talk. We talk about movement, *but* we do not get up and move! As the poster in my dentist's office says, it seems that "All our get up and go got up and went!"

As Christians, we have great good news to share. It is the good news of God's love and his Kingdom, and we must not settle down until we have shared the good news in every place on the face of the earth.

People

Jesus did not settle down in one place; neither did he

settle down with one group of people. Borrowing the words of Isaiah 9:1-2, Matthew says that Jesus went "In the direction of the sea, on the other side of Jordan, Galilee of the Gentiles!" Now "Galiliee" originally meant "circle" or "region," so "Galilee of the Gentiles" meant a "region of non-Jews." Obviously, Jesus was not going to settle down exclusively with members of his own racial background. He was going to keep moving until he had shared the good news with all people, irrespective of their racial or national background. Jesus was "a great light" for all the nations, and he had come to shine on all the people of the world who live in darkness.

This universal spirit of Jesus can be seen even in the selection of his disciples. Today's Scripture lesson tells us that Jesus called Simon (Peter) and his brother Andrew to come and follow him. Then, says the lesson, Jesus *"went on"* and called two other brothers, James and John. Jesus was always going on, always moving, even in the selection of his followers. He called some rough and tough fishermen, and then he "went on" later to call a rather sophisticated tax-collector. He called some, like Peter, who had volcanic tempers, and then he "went on" and called some others, like Andrew, who always seemed to be at peace. What a wonderful thing it is that all of us do not have to be alike in order to be called into the service of our Lord. Indeed, there is an advantage to our diversity, for with our different styles, we are better equipped to share the good news of God's love with all the different people of the world. We can not settle down until *all* the people have been reached.

In the biography of her mother, Eve Curie tells of her parents' decision to make their greatest discovery available to *all* humankind. When the therapeutic effects of radium became known, there was the temptation to exploit its use and availability for personal advantage.

Pierre Curie said to his wife Marie, "We have two choices. We can describe the results of our research without reserve, including the process of purification." Marie nodded her approval. "Or else," Pierre went on, "we can consider ourselves to be the proprietors, the 'inventors' of radium, patent the technique . . . and assure ourselves of rights over the manufacture of radium throughout the world."

Marie thought for a moment and then said, "It is impossible. It would be contrary to the scientific spirit . . If our discovery has a commercial future, that is an accident by which we must not profit. And radium is going to be of use in treating disease . . . It is impossible to take advantage of that."

The Curies were wise enough to see that their discovery of the healing possibilities of radium was a discovery that had to be shared with all the people of the earth.

So, too, must our discovery of God's loving Kingdom be shared with all the people of the earth. Like Jesus, we must not settle down and become too cozy with one group of people. We must keep on moving until we have shared the good news with *all* the people.

Program

Jesus did not settle down in one place or with one group of people. Neither did he settle down with one program.

I must say that this is something of a surprise to me. According to our Scripture lesson, the very first act of our Lord's public ministry was preaching. From the time that John the Baptizer was put into prison, says Matthew, "Jesus began to preach his message." And what a preacher he was! The best the world has ever seen! We would not have been surprised if Jesus had devoted his whole ministry exclusively to preaching.

Many lesser ministers have done that. The other night I went to a social get together for the ministers of this community. The spouses and families of the ministers were invited, and we all had a good time. It was not long, however, before the conversation centered on preaching, especially on the practice of preaching without notes. "How can a person preach without notes," someone asked. "You have to memorize the sermon," someone else answered. "That is what Dr. So-an-So, who is the Senior Minister of a large church in Washington, D.C., does. Of course that is all he does — preach — so he writes — and memorizes — every sermon, a sentence at a time."

I don't know if the report was accurate, and even if it was, one must remember that such large churches have a whole staff of ministers who share in the leadership of their multi-dimensioned programs. Nevertheless, I have known pastors who have tried to build a whole ministry on nothing but preaching. Jesus was not so vain. He was a great preacher, but he did not settle down with a program that was exclusively homiletical in nature.

Jesus preached, says Matthew, and then he *went on* to teach and to heal. "Jesus went all over Galilee, *teaching* in their synagogues, *preaching* the Good News of the Kingdom, and *healing* people from every kind of disease and sickness." (Matthew 4:23) Jesus had to keep on growing and keep on going until he had communicated the Good News of the Kingdom, not only through preaching, but also through teaching and healing and through every other conceivable program of ministry.

Pastoral counseling is good, but it is not enough by itself. Prayer meetings are good, but they are not enough by themselves. Involvement in programs of social reform is good, but it is not enough by itself. Missionary outreach is good, but it is not enough by itself. Preaching, teaching and healing are all good, but any one of them by itself is not enough.

You get the point: When Jesus applied himself to the

business of communicating the good news of God's love and Kingdom, he did not settle down into any one, limited program. He kept on moving until the Good News permeated every aspect and dimension and program of his life and ministry. Frankly, I do not see how we — and our whole congregation — can attempt to do any less.

The story of a college class that was graduating on a very lovely day, but a very hot and humid day, is appropriate at this point. As the graduates trooped across the platform and received their diplomas from the college president, he very graciously said to each one, "Congratulations." Then in a tone of voice that was more firm and less patient — for there was no point in prolonging this exercise on such a hot day — the president said sharply to each graduate: "Keep moving!"

That is what this sermon would say to each of you today: "Congratulations! but keep moving!"

So you have shared the Good News in your own house and in your own home town. Congratulations! But keep moving until you have shared it in every place.

So you have shared the Good News among your own people. Congratulations! But keep moving until you have shared it with all people.

So you have shared the Good News through some of your programs. Congratulations! But keep moving until you have shared it through all your programs.

Don't settle down until all people — everywhere — in every way that is possible — have heard the Good News of God's love!

God bless you. Amen.

God's Kind of Happiness

FOURTH SUNDAY AFTER EPIPHANY
Matthew 5:1-12

T. R. Glover said that Jesus promised three things to his followers: First, they would be entirely fearless; second, they would be absurdly happy; third, they would always be in trouble. It is that second item to which I want to call your attention: Jesus promises his followers — and that includes us — that they would be absurdly happy.

Dr. David James Randolph, senior minister of Christ Church, United Methodist, in New York City, preached a series of sermons on the National Radio Pulpit in late summer of 1976. The first sermon in that series was entitled "The Happy People." That was Dr. Randolph's description of the followers of Christ. They are God's happy people.

The other day I went to see one of our members who had recently been in the company of two of my minister friends. It was clear that she liked one of them better than the other. "You know them, don't you?" she said to me. "Yes," I replied. "Well," she said, "I call one of them Gloomy and I call the other one Glory." Sometimes we refer to people as "gloomy Christians," but that is a contradiction in terms. We cannot serve two masters, both gloom and glory. Jesus intended for us to radiate the glory of God in all our relationships. He intended for us to be his happy people.

Jesus himself was a happy person. He referred to

himself as the Bridegroom of the world. He actually had to defend himself from the accusations of his overpious critics and explain to the people why he and his disciples were so joyful. Even on the last night before his Crucifixion, he said, "These things I have spoken to you, that my joy may be in you, and that your joy may be full." (John 15:11 *The Good News Bible*)

Then, of course, Jesus gave us the Beatitudes, a list of nine ways to be happy. They are called the Beatitudes because originally each one of them began, "Blessed are . . ." But the Greek word that is translated as "blessed" may also be translated as "happy." Thus the Beatitudes describe a very special kind of happiness; they describe God's kind of happiness.

Today we are going to look at God's kind of happiness and try to see how it relates to our own lives.

Present

God's kind of happiness is a present experience. The Beatitudes are not pious projections of what shall be; they are the report of a present reality. I like the way William Barclay expresses this point in his *Daily Study Bible Series;* he says that the Beatitudes "are congratulations on what is." The happiness which is experienced by the Christian is not a happiness that is postponed until some future world of glory; it is a happiness that is experienced in the here and now.

So much of our worldly happiness is something we are always going to find just around the next corner. We are going to be happy, we say, just as soon as we get a good job or make a lot of money or get married or get divorced or get something else. But the action is always somewhere out in front of us, and we can never quite reach it. I am reminded of the parable of the donkey that had a long pole attached to his neck. A carrot was tied to the end of the pole, just a few feet in front of the donkey's mouth. You know what happened: as the donkey moved toward the carrot, the carrot remained an equal distance out in front of the animal's reaching mouth. In similar fashion, the happiness that is offered to us by the world is something that is always going to happen at some time in the future. But, to our dismay, it never actually happens.

I like the story of the preacher who met two little boys. After greeting them, he said, "Boys, would you like to go to heaven?" "Yes, sir!" one responded immediately. "No, sir," the other boy said honestly. Surprised by such honesty, the preacher asked, "Son, do you mean that eventually you don't want to go to heaven?" "I'd like to go *eventually,*" replied the boy, "but I thought you were getting up a load to go today." For many people, happiness — like heaven — is something that is going to come *eventually,* but it never quite arrives.

God's kind of happiness, on the other hand, the kind that God says we can have through our allegience to his Son, is a present reality. "Happy *are* those who know they are spiritually poor." "Happy are those who mourn." "Happy *are* those who are humble." Each one of the Beatitudes is in the *present* tense. Each one of them congratulates the Christian on the happiness he is already experiencing as a disciple of Jesus Christ.

George Matheson was a great preacher and hymn writer who lost his sight at an early age. He thought of that infirmity as his thorn in the flesh, as his personal cross. For several years, he prayed that his blindness would be removed. Like most of us, I suppose, he believed that personal happiness would come to him only *after* the handicap was gone. But then, one day God sent him a new insight: The creative use of his handicap could actually become his personal means of achieving happiness!

So, Matheson went on to write: "My God, I have never thanked Thee for my thorn. I have thanked Thee for my roses, but not once for my thorn. I have been looking forward to a world where I shall get compensation for my cross, but I have never thought of the cross itself as a present glory. Teach me the glory of my cross. Teach me the value of my thorn. Show me that I have climbed to Thee by the path of pain. Show me that my tears have made my rainbow."

Congratulations, George Matheson! Congratulations on finding God's kind of happiness — the kind of happiness that is not only a future hope, but also a very *present* reality.

So may it be for us all.

Permanent

God's kind of happiness is also a permanent experience. You will notice that each one of the Beatitudes is followed by an exclamation point. This indicates that the Beatitudes are triumphant shouts of a permanent joy that nothing in the world can ever take away.

Look for a moment at the word "permanent." It is composed of two Latin words: *per* which means "through" and *maneo* which means "to remain." Something that is permanent is something that remains through — endures — all times and all troubles and all assaults and all conditions. God's kind of happiness — the kind he wants each of us to enjoy — is permanent!

By contrast, most of our worldly happiness only lasts for a very short period of time. David Burpee, whose mail-order seed catalogues have brought pleasure to so many American gardeners, explained his own love of gardening in these words: "If you want to be happy for an hour, get drunk. If you want to be happy for a weekend, get married. If you want to be happy for a whole week, kill your pig and eat it. But if you want to be happy all your life, become a gardener."

If I remember correctly, when God created Adam and Eve, he hoped that all of us would be happy all our lives just by becoming his gardeners — his servants — his helpers. But we blew it! In any case, God's kind of permanent happiness stands in stark contrast to the poor, little, temporary pleasures that are offered to us by this world.

Wilhelm Von Humboldt wrote, "A man must seek his happiness and inward peace from objects which cannot be taken away from him." For us, this means that our only lasting happiness comes from God, through our personal relationship to his Son Jesus Christ.

Do you hear what I am saying and are you applying it to your own situation? We all have problems. We all have troubles. We all have handicaps, whether they are visible or not. Nevertheless, God can give us a kind of happiness that will *"remain through"* all these things.

The experience of General William Booth, the founder of the Salvation Army, illustrates this truth. Late in life Booth lost his sight, and his son Bramwell was sent to break the news to him that he would never see again. "You mean that I am blind," said the general. "I fear that we must contemplate that," his son answered. "I shall never see your face again?" asked the general. "No," said Bramwell, "probably not." The old man's hands moved across the blankets until they held his son's hands. "Bramwell," he said, "I have done what I could for God and the people with my eyes. Now I shall do what I can for God and the people without my eyes."

There was no resentment. There was no bitterness. There was only a deep-down joy — a deep-down happiness — that with eyes or without them, he could still serve his God and the people.

So may it be for us.

God's kind of happiness is present and permanent. It is also different.

Different

We have already implied some of the ways that God's kind of happiness is different from our own. But the difference is so radical that more should be said about it.

The point I want to make here is this: God's kind of happiness, as defined in the Beatitudes of our Lord, represents a radical reversal of almost everything we have ever been taught about the meaning of happiness!

Look at the Beatitudes again and contrast them with what we have been taught. "Happy are those who know they are spiritually poor." We have always been taught to define happiness in terms of wealth. "Happy are those who mourn." We have been taught that happiness means never experiencing anything that causes us grief. "Happy are those who are humble." We have been taught that happiness is defined in terms of aggression and the competitive spirit. "Happy are those whose greatest desire is to do what God requires." We have been taught that happiness lies in the desire to conform to the values of our own society.

"Happy are those who are merciful to others." We have been taught that the quality of mercy is a sign of weakness. "Happy are the pure in heart." Tell that one to the guys and gals at work! "Happy are those who work for peace." We have been taught that happiness is defined in terms of preparedness for war. "Happy are those who are persecuted because they do what God requires." We have tended to call such people fools or fanatics! "Happy are you when people insult you . . . and tell all kinds of evil lies against you because you are my followers." We tend to say, "Don't get mad, get even!"

We say it again: God's kind of happiness reverses

almost everything we have ever been taught about happiness. But if one of us has to be wrong — either us or God — you can be sure it isn't God!

Ralph Sockman wrote a book of sermons on the Beatitudes several years ago, and he called it *The Higher Happiness.* That title was so appropriate. God's kind of happiness is so much higher than ours that we can hardly comprehend it. When God's kind of happiness stands next to ours, it is like the World Trade Center towering over a tiny one-story bungalow! It is like a Rolls Royce parked next to a bicycle! It is like a majestic redwood tree looking down on a briar bush!

God's kind of happiness is so much greater than ours that it is tempting to use a completely different word for what God gives us — a word like joy or cheerfulness. This is what Beverly Sills, the great singer, was suggesting, I think, when she wrote: "I'm not happy; I'm cheerful. There's a difference. A happy woman has no cares at all. A cheerful woman has cares but has learned to deal with them."

I will confess my own bias. I prefer to stick with the word *happy,* but with this important reminder: The kind of happiness that God gives us through his Son, our Lord Jesus Christ, is infinitely greater than anything we have ever dreamed of!

When we realize our own utter and complete helplessness and come to God and put our whole trust in him, he receives us as members of his Kingdom and gives us that happiness which is so much higher than anything else.

In *Ruddigore,* a Gilbert and Sullivan opera, we are given the following advice:

> *If you wish in the world to advance*
> *Your merits you're bound to enhance,*
> *You must stir it and stump it,*
> *and blow your own trumpet,*
> *Or, trust me, you haven't a chance!*

May I suggest that our special task is blowing God's trumpet — trumpeting forth to the whole world a Christ-like God who gives his followers a very special kind of happiness, a happiness which begins now, a happiness that never ends!

If You've Got It — Flaunt It!

FIFTH SUNDAY AFTER EPIPHANY
Matthew 5:13-20

A few years ago, a product was advertised on television with the catchy slogan: "If you've got it, flaunt it!" I have forgotten the product but not the slogan!

I do have a vague impression that the product was a hair shampoo, and the sales pitch went something like this: If you have beautiful hair, you should not hide it, you should use a special shampoo that will highlight its beauty, and you should proudly display this beautiful head of hair to the whole world. In other words, if you've got it, flaunt it!

Why do I mention this slogan? Obviously, I am not selling hair products. I mention the slogan because it reminds me of today's Scripture lesson. Jesus seems to be saying: "If you've got faith, if God is alive in your life, if you are a Christian, then don't hide it; flaunt it!"

You Have Got It

You are beautiful people. Each and every one of you is a beautiful person. On a scale of one to ten, each one of you rates a ten! You've really got it.

This is not only my opinion. If I were the only one who rated you so highly, my opinion might be suspect. You might think I was bucking for a salary increase or that I was setting you up for some other big request. But I have absolutely nothing to ask of you.

As a matter of fact, I am only echoing the high opinion that Jesus has of you. He says, *"You* are the light of the world." He does not say that you might become the light of the world. He does not say that if you fulfill this requirement or that commandment, then you may be considered the light of the world. He says, *"You are* the light of the world." Since he had used the same title for himself on another occasion, he is rating you right up there beside himself. The writer of Genesis had said that you were created "in the image of God." The Psalmist said you were only "a little less than the angels." Now Jesus Christ is saying, "You are the light of the world." What a great claim! What a tremendous compliment! There is something of God in you, says Jesus. Truly, you are a beautiful person. There is no doubt about it; you've got it!

Russell Conwell traveled all over the world delivering his famous lecture which was titled, "Acres of Diamonds." The income from that lecture, incidentally, helped to build Temple University and Hospital in Philadelphia. The theme of the lecture, as I remember it, was that a man left his own property and traveled all over the world in search of great riches. He was not successful and returned to his own house as a poor and broken old man. How surprised he was to discover that one of the largest and richest diamond mines in the world was right there in his own back yard!

Some of us have spent our whole lives searching all over for God, and he was right there inside us all the time. His spirit is in us. His love is in us. His power is in us. His light is in us. That is why you are beautiful. That is why you rate a ten. This is why you have so much potential that you never even dared to dream of all your possibilities.

You are a great person because a great God is revealing himself in you and through you. You are a great person because something of the radiance of Jesus

Christ's personality is being reflected through your own life.

There is no doubt about it. You've got it! "You are the light of the world."

Flaunt It

Now, says Jesus, "If you've got it, flaunt it!" He tells us, "Let your light so shine before men, that they may see your good works . . ." Don't hide it. Don't cover it up. The nature of light, the purpose of light, is to shine. If you've got faith, don't hide it — spread it around. If you've got love, don't conceal it — express it toward others. God is within you. The Spirit of Christ is within you. Let your light shine. If you've got it, flaunt it.

Yet, the plain fact is that many of us do not flaunt it. We hide our light under a bushel basket. Our Christianity is the best kept secret in the world. The only time our faith becomes visible is when a crisis drags it out of us. Why are we so hesitant to flaunt the faith that is in us?

Part of the answer is contrariness. We simply will not accept Christ's estimate of us. We are too comfortable with the low level of our own self-esteem. We have become too friendly with our own sinfulness. Perhaps we enjoy feeling inferior because then people won't expect too much from us, and we will not have to disappoint them with our low-voltage performance. But whatever the reason, we are more contrary than "Mary, Mary," and we refuse to believe Christ when he says that we *are* the light of the world. We would be so much happier as persons and so much more effective as Christians if we would accept what Christ says about us and act on it, but we refuse.

Part of our hesitancy to flaunt the faith is explained by our psychological constitution. Some of us are timid. By nature, we are shy. We are hesitant to share our Lord and our faith with others because we are bashful. The only prescription I know of in such a case is practice, practice, and more practice.

Part of our hesitancy is explained by honest confusion. We remember that Jesus once told his followers to "pray . . . in secret" and not to let their left hands know what their right hands were doing. Some people wonder: Wasn't that Jesus' way of telling us that we should keep our faith a secret? No! It was not! Faith has a private dimension, to be sure. There are times when personal and private devotions are appropriate. But a major purpose of these private avenues to personal renewal is to increase the brightness and effectiveness of our faith in the public arena.

"Let your light shine," said Jesus. Your light is for everyone in the whole house!

Reasons for Flaunting Your Faith

So, let us look now at three reasons why we should flaunt the faith that is in us — why we should be more aggressive in sharing Christ with the world.

The first reason is competition. Those who have the faith should flaunt it, because it is for certain that those who don't have it flaunt it!

Some time ago, a major news magazine reported the birth of a new organization for bald-headed men and women. Its most famous members were actors: Telly Savalas, who starred for years as television's Detective Kojac, and Yul Brynner, who is currently making a comeback as the King in "The King and I." Rod Sterling may have become a member after he had his head shaved in order to star as Mussolini in a movie. The slogan of the organization affirms, "Bald is beautiful; if you *don't* have it, flaunt it!"

Many who are without faith, flaunt it. For years, Madeline Murray O'Hare made a career of it. Sensitive people cannot even look in the daily newspaper to see what is playing at the movies without being offended by the tasteless advertisements. Too many people openly brag about their faithlessness and agnosticism. The powers of light are engaged in a great struggle against the powers of darkness. Those who don't have the faith flaunt it. Therefore, those who do have the faith should flaunt it also, if only to keep the Christian option alive in the world today.

Second, if we have the light of God within us, we should flaunt it because someone else who is struggling along the way may see it and be inspired to keep going and/or to do better. Someone saw an old man planting some beautiful trees and asked him why he was doing it since it was clear that he would not live long enough to enjoy them. The old gentleman replied, "I will not be here, but my children and their children and other children will be here; I am doing it for them." Let your light shine! Affirm your faith. Plant your seeds. Even if it doesn't seem to be helping you, someone else will be inspired and benefit from your efforts.

Let me share a little ray of light with you — courtesy of Ira "Pete" Ennis. The people in my own congregation knew Pete very well. He died about three years ago, after a very long and very painful illness. I have known some brave people in my time, but I have never met a person who was more courageous than Pete. In very dark times, when the sun hid its face and refused to shine, Pete lived out the light that was in him.

His light is still shining for many of us, through a personal creed he dictated to his wife Mary shortly before his death. Pete wrote:

> *God never promised us we'd live forever or*
> *   that life would be easy.*
> *He does want us to take one day at a time and*
> *   make the most of it.*

Do the very best with each day that you can.
Work with what you have.
Give it your heart.
Don't worry about what you have no control
over.
God will take care of the rest.

I praise and thank God that Pete shared the light of his faith with the rest of us. It will surely encourage and help some others who are struggling along the same difficult and painful path that he traveled.

Finally, and most important, we should flaunt our faith — openly display it to the face of the world — so others will see it and "give glory to our Father who is in heaven." In the final analysis, a light has failed to fulfill its purpose if it has done nothing but call attention to itself. In a similar manner, we have failed as Christians if our activity — our "good works" — has done nothing but call attention to ourselves. Our purpose is to lead others to God.

Some of you remember the big blackout of 1965. A power failure in the northeastern part of the United States plunged over 30,000,000 people into total darkness. Interestingly, that crisis drew many people together into a camaraderie they had never known before. There was a lot of confusion, courage, humor, and adventure. The Long Island Railroad's 5:19 train from Pennsylvania Station ground to a halt about two miles west of Woodside, Queens. Finally, some of the passengers left the train, walked over hundreds of yards of dirt and stone and railroad ties and down four sets of wooden stairways, and headed toward Queens Boulevard. They were following a leader who carried a flashlight.

"Where are we going?" a woman asked her husband.

"We're just following the guy with the light," he answered. "I hope he's not some kind of nut headed for a cliff."

We live in a world where too many people are following too many "nuts" with flashlights who are headed for a cliff. Our job as Christian lights is to lead people out of the dangerous darkness to God.

What we do points others to a Source of Power that is far greater than ourselves. So it is said that in the heart of Africa a man, relieved of great pain by the surgical skill of a foreign doctor, looked up and asked, "But why have you come here to help us?" Albert Schweitzer simply answered, "The Lord Jesus sent me."

"Let your light so shine before men," said Jesus, "that they may see your good works and give glory to your Father who is in heaven."

Some people are following you, and they just pray you are not headed for a cliff. For God's sake, and for the sake of those who need whatever light and encouragement you are able to give them — if you've got it, flaunt it!

The Higher Righteousness

SIXTH SUNDAY AFTER EPIPHANY
Matthew 5:20-37

In Mark Twain's great story of Huckleberry Finn, Huck says, "What's the use you learning to do right when it's troublesome to do right and ain't no trouble to do wrong." Ole Huck sure had a way of putting his finger on the heart of a problem. We know we should do what is right, but it is so "troublesome." That is probably always true to some degree, but it was especially true of doing what is right as that was conceived by the Scribes and Pharisees of Jesus' day.

God had given his people some great principles by which to live. The Ten Commandments were such principles. They were broad guidelines that were to be applied to the individual situations in life. However, there arose a group of people called the Scribes who made it their business to reduce these great principles to thousands and thousands of very "picky" rules and regulations. For example, one of the principles said that no work was to be done on the Sabbath Day, for it was to be kept holy. Then the Scribes came along and defined "work" as carrying enough honey to put on a wound, carrying enough milk to drink one swallow, carrying enough ink to write two letters of the alphabet — and the definitions went on and on. Things got so ridiculous that people even argued over whether a man could wear his artificial teeth on the Sabbath!

Infractions of these rules, which were composed by

the Scribes and practiced by the Pharisees, brought on severe penalties. Huck Finn was correct. It had become very "troublesome to do right." Then Jesus came onto the scene and told his followers — and that includes us — that they were going to have to practice a better righteousness, a higher righteousness, than that of the Scribes and Pharisees. It is this higher righteousness that we want to focus on in this message.

Inward

The higher righteousness to which Jesus calls us is inward in nature. That is to say that it focuses on a person's inner desires, intentions and motives as much as on his outward acts. It specializes in exploring the secret areas of the heart.

The Scribes and Pharisees had focused on the prohibition of such outward acts as murder, adultery, and the swearing of oaths. Jesus did not remove that prohibition, but he carried the whole discussion back closer to its source and spoke in terms of anger, lust and telling the truth. Jesus turned the conversation outside in!

On another occasion, Jesus rebuked the Pharisees when they criticized his disciples for breaking one of the "rules" by eating in an improper manner. Jesus said, "Hear me, all of you . . . there is nothing outside a man which by going into him can defile him . . . For from within, out of the heart, come evil thoughts . . . murder, adultery . . . All these evil things come from within . . ." (Mark 7:14-23).

In our world, where we are so geared up to concentrate on the outward appearance of things — and to paint it, polish it, or put lipstick on it — we would do well to heed our Lord's warning to pay more attention to the inside of a person. To Jesus, thoughts are just as important as actions; desires are as important as deeds.

It is not enough to murder people, for example; we must not even be so angry at them that we would like to murder them. It is not enough not to commit adultery; we must not even look at another person with the kind of intense lust that would become an act if we had the opportunity. The higher righteousness of which Jesus speaks, and which the Kingdom of God requires, covers not only our outward behavior, but also our inner desires. God's claim to obedience is a total claim, involving the whole person in the entirety of his relationships.

I like the Chinese proverb which says,

> *If there is righteousness in the heart,*
> *there is beauty in the character.*
> *If there is beauty in the character,*
> *there will be harmony in the home.*
> *If there is harmony in the home,*
> *there will be order in the nation.*
> *When there is order in the nation,*
> *there will be peace in the world.*

Everything that is good in the world — and everything that is bad, for that matter — begins its journey on the inside of a person — in his dreams and desires and intentions. Therefore, that is where we should place our major emphasis. The Scribes and Pharisees didn't realize that. Jesus did. Hopefully, we do too.

Interventionist

The higher righteousness to which Jesus calls us is interventionist in nature. This is an unusual word, or at least an unusual use of a word, so I should explain what I mean by it. For example, an act like murder really involves a whole process. It begins as an angry thought, picks up steam by jelling into an attitude, really gets to rolling as it generates into angry words, and, finally, explodes into a violent act. You see the progression, don't you? Thought — attitude — words — actions. Jesus would have us intervene in this process at the very earliest stage and stop the potential murder when it is still only an angry thought.

Adultery probably involves a similar process. First, there is the lustful look, then the fantasizing and the fanning of the flame, then the outward act. Jesus wants us to intervene in the process and to put out the fire before someone actually gets burned.

The old adage that "the longest journey begins with a single step" also applies to such matters as murder and adultery. There is wisdom in not taking the first step if you already know that your final destination is not a worthy one. It is foolish to take the first drink if you can't stop until you are drunk. Just the other day, I heard a father tell his young son that "the best way to stop smoking was not to start." I don't want to sound too sticky or moralistic here, but I am convinced that we are talking about a sound principle. If you don't want a bad flower to grow, then try to nip it in the bud.

I am reminded of the time a young man went to evangelist Dwight L. Moody and told Moody of the terrible mess that he had made of his life. Then he asked, "Mr. Moody, what would you do if you were me?" Moody replied, "To begin with, I would not have permitted myself even to get into the mess you are in!" Well, Moody would not have won any prize as the world's most sensitive or sympathetic pastoral counselor! But again, he was operating on a sound principle. It was basically the same principle that Jesus recommends in Matthew 5:20-37, the principle of preventive medicine: The most effective way to stop some illnesses is to not let them get started.

Someone wrote:

> *Sow a thought, reap an act;*
> *Sow an act, reap a habit;*
> *Sow a habit, reap a character;*
> *Sow a character, reap a destiny.*

If the thought is unhealthy or destructive, then try to intervene in the process and stop it before you reap an unhappy destiny.

Impossible

The higher righteousness to which Jesus calls us is at least one more thing; in a very real way, it is impossible. You may be thinking, "Wow, what a disappointment! Why did the preacher mention all that other stuff, just to conclude that the whole enterprise is not possible?"

Well, hold on a minute and let's look at this point a little more closely. I say it is impossible, from a human point of view, to fulfill the higher righteousness to which Jesus calls us as his disciples.

Can any of us honestly say that we have never been angry at another person? Indeed, can any of us say that we have never "looked lustfully" at another person? Is it even humanly possible to completely refrain from these inner activities? I doubt it. We are not built that way. Even if we were, we would have to take into account the reality of sin.

I believe that Jesus realized the human impossibility of our accomplishing what he asked of us. At the same time, I believe that he wanted us to strive toward the goal he set for us, even if we never fully reached it. He knew that our unsuccessful efforts to "fulfill the Law" would eventually convince us of our human limitations and drive us back to the grace of Almighty God, the only One who, in the final analysis, can save us and make us truly righteous!

And who knows — who is so foolish that he sets limits

upon God in his dealings with us? When the disciples cried to Jesus, "Who then can be saved?" Jesus looked at them and said, "With men this is impossible, but with God all things are possible." (Matthew 19:26)

What we are saying is this: By our own human efforts, it is impossible to reach the higher righteousness to which Jesus summons us; but with God's help, all things are possible. So we keep on trying, not permitting our sin or shortcomings or guilt to overwhelm us, but moving onward and upward in response to the loving tug of God's grace on our lives.

As the great theologian, Huck Finn, said, "it's troublesome to do right and [it] ain't no trouble to do wrong." Sometimes, it seems more than "troublesome"; it seems downright impossible.

But hear this.

When Artur Rubenstein was in New York City one weekend and was invited to attend church, he replied, "Yes, I will go if you will take me to hear a preacher who will tempt me to do the impossible."

This morning, Jesus is "tempting" us to do the impossible: "For I tell you," he says, "unless your righteousness exceeds the Scribes and the Pharisees, you will never enter the kingdom of heaven."

Can You Love Someone You Don't Even Like?

SEVENTH SUNDAY AFTER EPIPHANY
Matthew 5:38-48

"I love him," she said, "but I really don't like him very much."

"That is very interesting," I said. "Can you tell me more of what you mean by that comment?"

"Well," she said, "I really do care about him and I really do want what is best for him. That is basically what I mean when I say that I love him. In many ways he is a terrific guy! But at the same time, I do not like the way he acts a lot of the time, and I disapprove of many of the things that he does. That is what I mean when I say that I don't like him very much. There are times when he is mean and selfish and small."

I have thought a lot about that woman's statement, and this sermon is largely the product of those thoughts. Was the woman merely expressing some sentimental and confused double-talk, or is it really possible to love someone you don't even like? We have got to come up with an answer to this question because Jesus tells us that we should love our enemies, and our enemies, by definition, are people we do not like.

Recently, I came across an interesting set of comments about our enemies. Here are a few of them:

Speak well of your enemies. Remember — you made them!

The best way to avoid enemies is to outlive them.

He hasn't an enemy in the world, but all his friends hate him.

If you can't love your enemies, compromise — forget them.

But we cannot always forget our enemies, and neither is there any guarantee that we will outlive them. We must find another strategy — a Christian strategy — for dealing with our enemies. We must try to understand what Jesus means when he tells us to love our enemies, and then we must try to do it.

Our starting point must come from somewhere beyond ourselves, for surely we are not capable of loving our enemies through our own unaided human effort. Our starting point must be rooted and grounded in the love of God — a love that is big enough to embrace both us and our enemies.

God Loves Everyone

The love of God is inclusive. There are no strings attached to it. It does not pick and choose. It is not contingent upon our good behavior or the quality of our character. As Matthew puts it, the love of God is like the sun that shines on those who are evil *and* on those who are good; the love of God is like the rain that is poured on those who are just *and* on those who are unjust.

There is a song we sing which says, "Red, yellow, brown or white; they are precious in his sight. Jesus loves the little children of the world." And the big children, too! God is an Equal Opportunities Employer: He does not exclude anyone on the basis of race, creed, color, nationality, sex, or any other category you can think of. God loves everyone.

God even loves his enemies. At least that is what I understand Matthew to be saying when he says that God makes the sun to rise on the evil and sends the rain on the unjust. For love, as Matthew means it, is basic kindness and benevolent good will. It is providing for the welfare of another person, even when you don't like the other person or the other person doesn't like you. Therefore, when God sends the sun and the rain on those who are evil and unjust, he is expressing his great love for them, even though he may not like them or approve of what they are doing.

I have the feeling that Jesus did not like the money-changers very much when he took a whip and drove them out of the temple, saying that they had turned God's house of prayer into a den of thieves. I have the feeling that Jesus didn't like the Pharisees very much when he referred to them as hypocrites. Nevertheless, he loved these people. He did not approve of what they were doing, but he genuinely wanted what was best for them. Eventually, he would give his life on a cross to prove his love for them.

The name and the nature of God is love, and he expresses his basic kindness and benevolent good will toward us even when we are not very likeable! He loves us even when we break his heart.

God may not like us sometimes, but he always loves us! That is where we must begin as we try to respond to Jesus' directive that *we* should love *our* enemies.

God Wants Us to Be Like Him

It would sound almost blasphemous to say it if Matthew had not said it first: God expects us to be like him! That is what Jesus meant when he told us to "become sons of your Father in heaven." In fact, the whole motivation for loving our enemies is that we may become the children of God. That is a biblical way of telling us that we are to be like God.

Recently, my son John Thomas, who is seven years old, and sometimes seems to be going on twenty, was a greeter at the church. He shook the hands of people and welcomed them as they came into the worship service. As I entered the sanctuary, he shook my hand and said, "We are glad to have you here this morning, sir; and what is your name?" "My name is John Thomas Randolph," I said. He replied, "Well, isn't that a funny coincidence; that is my name too." The son is like his father, both in his name and, I could add, in his sense of humor!

To be a "son of your Father in heaven" is to be like God.

Since God loves even his enemies, to be like him we must love our enemies, too.

This is hard stuff we are talking about here. It is easy to talk about, but very hard to do. Our natural inclination is to love our friends and to hate our enemies. Our natural inclination is to take "an eye for an eye and a tooth for a tooth." We operate on the basis of the law of "Tit for Tat." If someone strikes us, we want to hit him back, and we want at least equal justice for any injury done to us.

However, there is no virtue in such an approach, says Jesus. Even pagans can do that! More — much more — is expected of us as Christians. We are expected to be like God in that we are to love even our enemies, to will and to work for what is best for them. We are to love those we don't even like.

About all I can do at this point is to offer a brief prayer: *HELP!* Lord, if you want us to love those we don't even like, then I surely hope and pray that you will give us a practical and helpful strategy to accomplish what you want.

According to Matthew, that is precisely what Jesus has already done.

A Practical Strategy

The strategy that Jesus has given us is prayer. "Pray

for those who persecute you," says Jesus. How do we get to the point where we can love our enemies? We pray for them. How do we get to the point where we can actually love those we don't even like? We pray for them.

Praying for our enemies really does two things.

1. It transforms our feelings of hatred into more positive and creative impulses.

The practical fact of the matter is that we cannot continue to hate someone we pray for. When we honestly bring ourselves and the "enemy" into the prayerful presence of God, the whole situation is changed and we are changed. Someone has said that the best way to get rid of an enemy is to get rid of enmity, and that is what prayer accomplishes.

Glenn Clark, who was an expert on prayer, wrote, "The man who learns and practices the laws of prayer should be able to play better, to work better, to love better, to serve better, for to learn how to pray is to learn how to live." All of what Clark says is good, but here is the thought we are concentrating on right now: The person who learns how to pray is able to love better.

2. Prayer not only transforms our hate into love or positive good will; it also may transform the person for whom we pray.

Prayer may bring the power of God into a situation in such a way that someone who was once our enemy actually becomes a friend!

I like the story of the small boy who was saying The Lord's Prayer one evening before he got into bed. He was overheard to say: "And forgive us our debts as we forgive those who are dead against us." He may not have had all the right words, but he sure was on the right track! Prayer — or rather God entering our lives through prayer — gives us the power to forgive and to love even those who are dead against us!

The differing approaches of Confucius and Lao-tse illustrate this point. Confucius taught his followers to "recompense injury with justice and recompense kindness with kindness." But Lao-tse, the founder of Taoism, wrote, "Recompense injury with kindness. To those who are good to me, I am good, and to those who are not good to me, I am also good. Thus all get to be good." Let me say, emphatically, that Lao-tse came much closer to the teaching of Jesus on this matter than did Confucius.

William Jennings Bryan, the famous orator, told a story that confirms the fundamental wisdom of Jesus. It was the story of a farm boy who, after several months of bashfulness, finally said to the girl he loved: "Mary, I've been loving you for a long time. I am not very good at talking, but will you be my wife?" Mary replied, "Yes, John, I've been loving you, too. I'll be happy to be your wife." Later that night when John was alone, he looked up at the stars and was heard to say, "O Lord, Mary loves me and I ain't got nothing against nobody now." When we know that God or at least one other person loves us — really deep-down, honest-to-goodness loves us — then we "ain't got nothing against nobody" else. When we are deeply loved by someone else, then it becomes much easier for us to act in loving ways toward others.

Therefore, let us pray for our enemies, even as Jesus counseled us to do. It will help us and it may even transform the person for whom we pray; it may get rid of an enemy by changing him into a friend!

"I love him," she said, "but I really don't like him very much."

Is that possible?

Yes, it is possible to love someone we don't even like.

Let me make one quick suggestion. During this coming week, pick out one person whom you don't like very much. Then pray for that person and honestly try to love that person, as we have spoken of love in this sermon.

Who knows? You may even start to like him!

Worry Is a Waste!
Three Ways to Stop It

EIGHTH SUNDAY AFTER EPIPHANY
Matthew 6:24-34

In his book, *Your Erroneous Zones*, Dr. Wayne Dyer describes worry and guilt as the two "great wastes" of life. Guilt will have to stand in line and wait its turn to be the subject of another sermon. Worry is the subject of this one.

Worry is a waste. An old Chinese proverb says: "The legs of the stork are long, and the legs of the duck are short. You cannot shorten the legs of the stork, nor can you lengthen the legs of the duck. Why worry?" That sounds something like Jesus in today's Scripture lesson when he asks: "Which one of you can live a few years more by worrying about it?" No one, of course. Worrying about life will not prolong life. On the contrary, too much worry will probably send us to an early grave.

Worry is a waste. It burns up a lot of our time and energy, but it never accomplishes anything that is positive and good. In fact, most of the things we worry about never happen. Dr. Greatheart, a character in one of Alistair MacLean's sermons, gave this advice to one of his sons as the boy was leaving home and starting out on life's great adventure: "Johnny, the thing to do, my lad, is to hold your own end up, and to do it like a gentleman, and please remember the biggest troubles you have got to face are those that never come."

It might be a helpful exercise for us to copy the woman who realized that her worries were ruining her life, so she made herself a "worry table." In analyzing her worries, she came up with these figures:

40% — will never happen; worry is the result of a tired mind.
30% — about old decisions which I cannot alter.
12% — others' criticism of me, most untrue, made by people who feel inferior.
10% — about my health, which gets worse as I worry.
 8% — legitimate, since life has some real problems to meet.

Worry is a waste. It wastes our time, our energy and our health. What are we to do about it?

Several years ago, the Hayden Planetarium decided to have some fun and to educate the public at the same time, so it offered to take reservations for imaginary space trips. The sponsors were shocked when applications rolled in by the thousands. Finally, someone concluded that so many people applied for the trips because they wanted a chance, though it was only an imaginary one, to escape from all their troubles and worries. Indeed, one applicant wrote: "It would be heaven to get away from this troubled earth and to go some place where I wouldn't have to worry."

Let me quickly say, before you buy a ticket for Mars, that we cannot run away from our worries. The worry is within us, and if we are to get rid of it, we must attack it at the source. Changing our location will not get rid of our worry; changing our attitude will get rid of it. At least, that is what I understand Jesus to be telling us in today's Scripture lesson. As we look at the lesson closely, Jesus is actually suggesting three ways to stop worrying.

Affirm Your Worth

The first way to stop worrying, says Jesus, is to recognize and affirm our worth. After telling us not to be worried about such things as food and drink and clothes, and reminding us of God's care for the birds, Jesus goes on to ask, "After all, isn't life worth more than food? and isn't the body worth more than clothes? . . . Aren't you worth much more than birds?" I must confess to you that this is the first time I have ever heard of anyone linking a discussion of worry to the matter of worth. I only noticed the connection this time because of the particular way that *The Good News Bible* translates the words of our Lord.

Jesus showed great wisdom when he pointed out the relationship between our worry and our estimates of self-worth. When you stop to think about it, those persons who are convinced of their value and importance as individuals very seldom, if ever, worry. Those people who worry the most are those people who feel they are unimportant, insignificant, and of very little worth. I think of Oscar LeVant, the gifted musician and writer, who freely admitted that he worried himself into several major illnesses. Surely, it is no accident that LeVant entitled his autobigraphy, *The Unimportance of Being Oscar.*

Jesus affirms that we are of great worth to God. God values the birds of the air and the flowers of the field, and he takes care of them and provides for their needs. Surely, God values us more than the birds and the flowers, and he will take care of us and provide for our needs. There is no legitimate need for us to worry.

God has invested too much love in us not to provide for our needs. He does not want us to be wasted away through worry. I like the story of the Chinese wife who said to her husband, "I would like a new coat." Her husband said to her, "What will you do with your old coat?" She replied, "I will make a bed cover out of it." He asked, "What will you do with your old bed cover?" She answered, "I will make pillowcases out of it." He said, "What will you do with the old pillowcases?" She responded, "I will make cleaning clothes." He said, "What will you do with the old cleaning clothes?" She said, "I will tie them together and make a mop out of them." He continued, "What will you do with the old mop?" She answered, "I will chop it up into little pieces, mix it with cement, and in the springtime we will use it to patch the holes in our cottage." "All right," he said, "you may have a new coat."

That which is of worth is durable and it will be preserved! We are of worth to God and he will take care of us and use us for his purposes. Therefore, says Jesus, there is no need for us to worry.

Concentrate on Today

The second way to stop worrying, says Jesus, is to concentrate on living one day at a time: "So do not worry about tomorrow; it will have enough worries of its own. There is no need to add to the troubles each day brings."

Jesus is not forbidding us to participate in normal, intelligent, common-sense planning for the future. He is telling us that we should not try to live two days at the same time, today *and* tomorrow, and he is telling us not to worry anxiously about that which has not yet happened. Life has to be divided into manageable proportions, with our emphasis upon those tasks which are immediately at hand.

When Dr. Clovis Chappell was a young man, he attended Webb School and studied Latin. He was ashamed to enter the beginning class, where he really belonged, because he was so much older than the other students; so he entered an older and more advanced class that was reading Caesar. It was a humiliating experience, and he had been in the class for ten whole weeks before he answered a single question. He was quite worried about the situation. Then the wise headmaster, who was called Old Sawney, took him aside and gave him some good advice: "If you will learn just one word a day, you will go to the head of the class." Chappell followed the advice and by the end of his second year, he was, in fact, the best student in his class.

Thomas Carlyle labored for a long time to write the history of the French Revolution. It was his greatest work and he hoped that it would rescue him from poverty and bring him the literary success he wanted. When he had finished writing the first volume, he took it to John Stuart Mill to read. Mill was very impressed, but when he went to bed that night, he left the loose pages of the manuscript scattered on the floor by his chair. The next morning, his maid, thinking they were papers he had discarded, used them to start a fire!

To say that Carlyle was worried would be to put it mildly; he was a depressed and defeated man. He did not have the will to start over. He vowed he would never write again. For days and days, he brooded and worried over his misfortune. Then one day he looked out the window and saw a man building a brick wall. He watched as the man picked up one brick at a time and put it in place.

As Carlyle watched, he stopped worrying; he decided he would be able to write his book again. He didn't have to worry about writing the whole book all at once. He would write the book one page at a time. That was possible. That was manageable. He could do that. Thus it was that he overcame his worry by dividing life into manageable proportions and concentrating on the task that was immediately at hand.

One day at a time, one step at a time, one word at a time, one brick at a time, one page at a time — that is the second way to stop the waste of worrying.

Focus on Our Faith

The third way to stop worrying, says Jesus, is to focus on our faith in God and not on our problems. What is your problem? Are you worried about having enough food to put on your table? Are you worried about having enough clothes to keep you warm? Are you worried about having enough fuel to get you through the winter? Don't worry about these things, says Jesus. "Instead, give first place to (God's) Kingdom and what he requires, and he will provide you with all these other things."

Here is where we run head on into the major problem with worry. Fundamentally, worry is a lack of faith in God. Worry is not caused by outward circumstances, although outward circumstances may aggravate worry once it has already started. Worry is not basically a psychological problem, although it may have harmful emotional side effects. Worry is not basically a sociological problem, although it can upset a whole community. Worry is basically a loss of faith in God; an inability or an unwillingness to trust God to provide for our needs.

That is why it is so important to focus on God and not on our problems. When we focus on our problems, it is inevitable that our worry will increase. That is "the nature of the beast." But when we focus on God, we are acting on faith, and the whole cause of our worry is eliminated!

I will admit to you that I am preaching to myself now, as well as to you. I find it much easier to focus on my problems than on the Problem-Solver. I find it much easier to focus on my fears than on my faith. I find it much easier to focus on my worries than on the Word. I suspect that you do, too. Therefore, it is all the more important that we adopt the strategy of Jesus and begin to move in the opposite direction.

Dr. Norman Vincent Peale tells of a personal

experience that illustrates exactly what we are talking about. Once he was scheduled to speak at a large convention. He arrived in town in the afternoon and began to get a bad case of laryngitis. He called a doctor who came to his hotel and, at Peale's direction, sprayed his throat and gave him some pills.

Then the doctor said, "Now I would like to give you the treatment that can really heal you." "What is it?" asked Peale. "Why did you wait so long?"

"Because," the doctor said, "I didn't think I would have to give it to *you*. It is called the golden key. The golden key is this: Focus your thoughts on God; don't focus them on your problem. You have been focusing on your problem! That tightens up your nervous system so the blood doesn't flow harmoniously. As a result, you experience sickness. Stop focusing on the problem, and start focusing on God."

The key worked. Dr. Peale writes: "When I walked to the platform to speak that night, I testify that my voice was never stronger than it was that night."

How do we stop worrying — and start living and performing in ways that are more creative and effective than we thought were possible? We focus our attention on God, not on our problems.

Worry is such a waste! It wastes our time, our energy, and our health. Jesus tells us that we can stop our worrying when we recognize and affirm our worth; when we apply ourselves to the tasks immediately at hand; and when we focus our thoughts on God instead of our problems.

May it be so for us.

What Goes Up Must Come Down

TRANSFIGURATION OF OUR LORD
Matthew 17:1-9

A little boy was out in his backyard, throwing a ball up in the air. An elderly passerby, not accustomed to such youthful delights, asked the boy what he was doing. He replied, "I am playing a game of catch with God. I throw the ball up in the air and he throws it back."

I am in no position to comment on God's ability to play ball, but I do know that whatever goes up must come down. There may be exceptions, such as Charlie Brown's kite! But as a rule, whatever goes up must come down. The process is so predictable that you could refer to it as a scientific law. The same process applies to our religious lives. It is a good thing to "go up" to a great experience with God, but we will become greatly disillusioned if we do not remember that eventually we have to "come down" again.

Wonder

I believe that is what happened to Peter, James and John on the Mount of Transfiguration. Their experience was a religious "high"; it was a thing of marvelous wonder. There on the slopes of Mount Hermon, God revealed to them that Jesus was his Son, the Christ. Just as God had revealed himself to Moses on Mount Sinai, he now revealed the true identity of his Son on Mount Hermon. For one shining moment at least, the disciples knew beyond a shadow of a doubt that Jesus was the Christ, the long-awaited Messiah, and their personal Lord. You can almost see the excitement on Peter's face as he exclaims, "it is wonderful for us to be here." (J. B. Phillips)

Any experience in which we recognize Jesus as the Son of God and our personal Lord is a Transfiguration experience. It may take place as we stand on the slopes or the summit of a mountain; it may take place as we stand or kneel on a wooden floor at sea level. It may take place in a service of worship like the one we are in right now. But wherever it happens, God is dramatically real to us, and we know beyond a shadow of a doubt that Jesus Christ is our personal Savior and Lord. It is a wonderful experience.

Can you think of any experience that you have had that was characterized by the same soul-stirring sense of wonder that characterized the experience of Peter, James and John on the Mount of Transfiguration? Perhaps the closest I ever got to that experience was one night at our church camp when, as a high school student, I lighted a candle that represented my first commitment to the full-time (ordained) ministry and then set the floating tray that held that candle out on the soft waves of the Chester River. They called it a "Galilean Service" in those days, but for me it was a religious "high." The Jesus I had heard of in Sunday School and church "became" the Christ, the Son of God, and my personal Leader. I saw no clouds that represented the presence of God. I heard no voices. Moses and Elijah were not visibly present to signify the Law and the prophets. But it was a wonderful experience, and as those candles moved on out into the river, I caught, for a moment at least, "the shining possibilities" of a life that is lived under the Lordship of Jesus Christ.

You know, every time I come into a worship service like this one, I pray that something like that will happen to someone who is present. We all need such moments of high religious experience.

Fear

But, my brothers and sisters, you can be sure of this: The sense of wonder will almost always be followed, soon or late, by a sense of fear. When we really perceive the holiness of God standing before us in the presence of Jesus Christ, it is a terrifying thing. We may or may not "fall on our faces" as did Peter, James and John, but we are filled with fear. It is a fear that is brought to birth by the realization that we are sinful persons who are now standing in the presence of the holy God. The contrast is overwhelming and frightening.

I think of the young Martin Luther, fourteen years of age, looking at the totally committed life of Prince William of Anhalt and saying, "No one could look upon him without feeling ashamed of his own life." No one of us can look upon the holiness of God without feeling ashamed of his or her life.

Remember Isaiah. In the year that King Uzziah died, he saw the Lord, high and lifted up in the temple, and he cried, "Woe is me! For I am lost; for I am a man of unclean lips, and I dwell in the midst of a people of unclean lips; for my eyes have seen the King, the Lord of hosts." (Isaiah 6:5)

I am not advocating that we kick ourselves and go around confessing, even bragging, what miserable sinners we are. There is no profit in that. It bores other people nearly to death! And it magnifies all the negative forces within us which are really part of the problem.

I am only suggesting that we get a realistic estimate of ourselves when we stand in the presence of the God whose holiness is incarnated in Jesus, the Christ. Here is the marvelous thing. Here is the good news. The God whom we feared would strke us dead because of our terrible wickedness turns out to be our Friend!

Christ walks over to us, as he did to the disciples on the Mount of Transfiguration, and he says, "Do not be afraid." But what does he mean by that? Did he mean that we should not be afraid of problems and obstacles in life because he will help us to overcome them? Did he mean that we should not be afraid of illness because he is our Great Physician? Did he mean that we should not be afraid of death because he has conquered it on our behalf? Did he mean that we should not be afraid of death because he has taken away its power to destroy us? Did he mean that we should not be afraid to live and to love and to face life openly because he is with us? I have no doubt that all these things are true, but I do not think that is what Christ meant *in this particular passage.*

Rather, he was saying, "Do not be afraid *of me!* I know your sinfulness, but I also know your possibilities, and I love you and forgive you. I am your Lord; I am also your Friend." As Suzanne deDietrich says: "To those who acknowledge their unworthiness, God always shows his merciful face."

Engagement

But as we said, whatever goes up must come down, and perhaps we have been on this mountain for long enough today. I pray we have caught something of the wonder of the God who revealed himself in his Son, Jesus Christ. I pray that we have experienced something of the forgiving Friendship of Christ that overcomes our fear. But in any case, we must go down from this mountain.

When we have high moments of religious experience, it is always a temptation to try to prolong them. That is why Peter wanted to build three booths; he wanted to settle down on a great religious experience and try to live on it forever. One of the most frustrating problems many pastors have is trying to deal with people who have had a great religious experience — a dramatic conversion, for example — and then get angry at the pastor and the local church because they can't keep on cranking out these experiences of religious "highs" every time the church opens its doors. No pastor or local church can live up to the expectations of these people because the expectations are unrealistic and unhealthy. They are also "unscientific" because they ignore the principle that whatever goes up must also come down.

I was going to call this sermon "Up the Mountain — Down the Mountain" because the first verse of our Scripture lesson says that Jesus led his disciples "up a high mountain" and the last verse of our Scripture lesson says the "disciples came down the mountain." What goes up must come down!

Sometime ago, I turned on the television set and saw part of an interview with a man named Wickwire. I missed his first name, but Mr. Wickwire was being interviewed because he had successfully climbed a mountain that is known as K-2. It is located near the China border and is considered a greater challenge than Mt. Everest. There were many exciting scenes of Mr. Wickwire and his adventures on the mountain. But — here is the point — the interview was conducted in Mr. Wickwire's office as he sat behind his desk dressed in a business suit. Wickwire went up the mountain, but eventually he had to come down the mountain. We all do, and it doesn't make any difference whether the mountain is a real physical mountain or the figurative mountain of religious experience.

When I shared the idea for this sermon with Ruth Schueler, our church secretary, she said, "You know, I guess that is the explanation for much of our drug culture. Young people who use drugs think they have to be 'high' all the time. They don't seem to realize that life has it's 'lows,' too. At least that is my opinion." Many of us would agree with Ruth's opinion.

There is human need at the foot of the mountain. The first thing that Jesus and his disciples encountered when they came down from the mountain was a distraught father who was seeking help for his epileptic son. Only the Lord knows what else they encountered, although I imagine that if we would really open our eyes and look right around ourselves right here in our own town, we would pretty much see the same things that Jesus and his disciples encountered. Getting engaged in genuinely concerned efforts to minister to these situations in ways that are helpful and healing is a necessary part of our commitment to Jesus Christ.

As Halford Luccock expressed it, we need to develop "the fine art of going downhill." So much of our lives is devoted to going "uphill," to getting ahead, to upward mobility, to moving "up town." But after we have been high on the mountain of religious experience, we need to develop the art of going downhill so we can use our newly strengthened faith to help others — in Christ's name.

"The bear went over the mountain to see what he could see," says the nursery rhyme. And all he could see was "the other side of the mountain." Well, the "other side" of the mountain of wondrous religious experience is unselfish, sacrificial helpfulness to others. In marriage, the honeymoon always follows the engagement, but in terms of Christian service, the order is reversed. When the honeymoon on the mountain is over, then comes the engagement with human need in the valley.

So — throw your ball into the air, and God will throw it back. "That is the way the ball bounces," as they say.

Whatever goes up must eventually come down!

And — up or down — Christ is with us!

Wesley Theology wanted Clarity.
Plain Truth for Plain People
Corp. of Wesley Theology easy
    to identify —

1. Justification & Sanctification
   Christian Perfection.
   Colin Williams Book on Wesley
       Theology —
Problem: Slow to spell out his
                Doctrine
Conversion — Hall mark
what is Real Christian / ceding?
   A Restoration of Man to Image
       of God
Letter to Rev. John Taylor:
Conversion — Not just change of
                        status
But actual change.